FOREWORD

When I walked into an Irish Football Association meeting room in late spring 2019, for my interview for the Northern Ireland senior women's team manager's role, little did I know what the appointment and the journey might hold in the subsequent three years.

The atmosphere in the room resonated with what I wanted it to become. It was tailor made for me. Perhaps because of the backdrop, looking out on our international stadium, it got my joy glands moving. What would I not give to occupy that dugout again representing my country.

Following my interview that afternoon, I and my good friend Jim Grattan had arranged to meet for a catch-up.

No sooner had we sat down for a coffee than I had to take two phone calls. The first one was from Michael Boyd telling me I had got the job and the second one was from a Scottish club offering me a head coach job in the Scottish Premiership. It was like the proverbial bus. You wait ages for one to come along and then two arrive at the same time.

I thought of what my parents would have told me – to never go back on your word. So it was Northern Ireland Women for me.

My first official match in charge was a Euro qualifier against Norway at Seaview. Naturally, the first thing I did was to do research on Norway and I quickly realised how huge they were, and are, in the women's game, having previously won both the Euros and the World Cup.

When the squad met up it was great to get together, especially with the existing staff. They provided me with a rundown on the players, which gave me an insight into the demands that lay ahead.

I was told our best player could only last 60 minutes, that someone in midfield could not head the ball and a great player had a "gammy knee". Then I was told another player needed cortisone injections to help her through games, while another top player had missed in excess of 50% of games because of injuries.

Having worked so long in the professional game, by this stage I was starting to wonder what I had let myself in for. I was thinking about finding that phone number from Scotland!

It soon dawned on me that these negative connotations of injuries, restrictions etc had to be removed if we were going to reach our true potential.

And that's what we set out to do as we aimed to turn the team's fortunes around - and the players bought into it.

Worse was to come in terms of injuries unfortunately. Demi Vance damaged an anterior cruciate ligament (ACL), which is a 10-month rehab case. Megan Bell was going to be out for two years. We lost Abbie Magee to the dreaded ACL. The list went on and on.

Sam Kelly, Caragh Hamilton, Vicky Carleton and Danielle Maxwell would all miss the Euros through injury.

The selection process was difficult along the way as everybody now wanted to be part of our upward trajectory.

The hardest part for me was telling players they weren't in the squad for the Euros in England.

A NEW DREAM

This is the ultimate underdog story: the story of a team who were resigned to operating in the backwaters of women's international football before an inspirational figure instilled belief and passion in them.

Players who had pulled on the green jersey year upon year, campaign after campaign, never dreamt they could reach the heights of appearing at a major tournament.

That was until Kenny Shiels came along and sparked a new dream.

He was a coach who had been there and done that in several countries, winning plenty of trophies along the way.

Shiels had successfully managed a Northern Ireland international boys' team in the past but he was keen to bring his know-how to the senior international stage.

The veteran manager immediately set about reinvigorating the experienced players in the squad which he inherited — and introducing younger players who could step up to a higher level.

He found a blend that worked. And he moulded a togetherness which the players often describe as "one big family".

Flanked by his son Dean, goalkeeping coach Dwayne Nelson and a strong backroom team, he instilled a hunger and drive that led to a maiden appearance at a major tournament.

Through words and the brilliant pictures of William Cherry this book charts, in chronological order, Northern Ireland's incredible journey to UEFA Women's Euro 2022 - often against the odds - and the part the senior women's team played in the record-breaking tournament in England.

Enjoy!

Nigel Tilson

The more senior players were worrying me. I couldn't sleep at night. There were five players who realistically would never have a chance of playing in a major finals again: Marissa (Callaghan), Ashley (Hutton), Julie (Nelson), Furney (Rachel Furness) and Mac (Sarah McFadden).

These five and many others had given so much to be part of our team.

And many people had supported them along the way, making major sacrifices to help them.

I became obsessed with their wellbeing. I was also obsessed with the 'what if?' alongside this because I had to put the team first.

Talking of making sacrifices, my backroom staff travelled the country and helped me with sessions in a voluntary capacity to help the girls.

Dean (Shiels) and Dwayne (Nelson) were hands on with sessions on Saturday mornings and travelling to Moyola Park and Jordanstown, giving up their nights to improve the sharpness, fitness and duty of care for the players.

A lot of hard work and preparation went in to the girls' improvement, and we were faced with massive challenges along our pathway to Southampton. But we got there.

We couldn't have done it without our entire backroom staff, our association, our comms team, our administration and the media.

I reflect now on those three years and feel so honoured and proud of what everybody has achieved.

And it would be great to do it all over again.

Kenny Shiels
Manager
Northern Ireland Senior Women's Team

DREAMS DO COME TRUE...

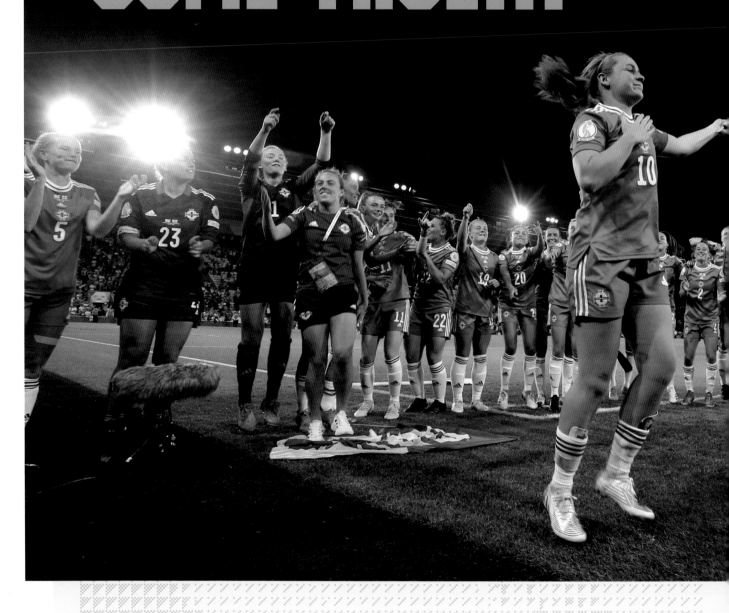

Friday 30 August 2019 was an inauspicious day for the revolution to begin. Our senior women's team were at Seaview at home to Norway in the opening game of the UEFA Women's Euro qualifiers.

One 6-0 defeat later we were on the way to Rodney Parade in Newport to take on a full of confidence Welsh team.

Maybe we went more in hope than expectation, but when Simone (Magill) put us ahead after 10 minutes the hope rose.

Our players matched Wales and grew in stature before our eyes. Hard to believe when the added time board went up that Wales were 2-1 up. No matter. Demi (Vance) swung a last minute free-kick right under the crossbar and there was Ashley (Hutton) on her 100th cap to head the ball over the line for a precious point. We were up and running, and with belief.

The away trip to Stavanger in November 2019 was as painful as the home game against Norway but then we more than matched Wales in Belfast in a 0-0 draw.

At this point the door to the Euro finals opened a little. If we could win our next four games we would be in the play-offs. And if you're in the play-offs, you can see the finals from there! This was A New Dream in the making.

Covid-19 struck everywhere as 2020 dawned, and it wasn't until September of that year that the qualification campaign resumed.

A tricky away pair of matches started in Torshavn where the Faroe Islands were beaten 6-0.

Probably the pivotal game of the whole campaign came next as we took on Belarus in Minsk.

With Jackie (Burns) sent off early doors we were down to 10 players for more than an hour. Again no matter. A Demi corner and a Furney (Rachel Furness) header brought the points safely back to Belfast.

Seaview beckoned again in November. The home qualifier against Belarus was a nervous one. The New Dream was well under way but maybe the squad realised the magnitude of the occasion. It was 3-2 to us on the night though.

Then it was Faroe Islands at home, and the players were in determined mood. The Faroes went home beaten 5-1 and history had been made with a play-off place secured!

This was indeed new territory and so was Kovalivka, an hour from Kiev, when we drew Ukraine in the play-offs. Furney and Simone gave us a 2-1 away lead, but Furney came back home with her leg in a cast after a fracture. Again no matter.

Back to Seaview for the final time in the campaign three days later. Marissa (Callaghan) stretched our lead and Nadene (Caldwell) sent the goalkeeper so far the wrong way in the final minute of added time she almost had to pay to get back in to the ground.

Added to this was the WWE-style body check on Sarah Mac (McFadden) which generated some red card comedy, and we were going to the Euros!

To give the achievement some context, 47 of UEFA's 55 national associations started the qualification tournament. We were seeded 32nd at the outset, and 15 of the top 16 seeds made it to the finals. Some achievement, and A New Dream for everyone.

The finals were delayed by a year due to the pandemic, however the excitement was real as we descended on Manchester for the draw. Our opponents were unveiled. Norway again, Austria and a huge roar from the crowd when we drew host nation England.

All three of our group matches were to be played in sunny Southampton which would allow the GAWA to have a fantastic base camp.

After that July 2022 came round very quickly and our collective pride reached its peak on Thursday 7 July just before 8pm when Sarah led our senior women's team out for their first ever game in a major tournament finals.

We were there as an equal partner on merit and no-one will ever tell us differently.

This book is the story of the journey from Seaview to Southampton with many stops in between.

It's the story of how we all dreamed A New Dream and the story of how the next generation of our girls and boys are now making their own dreams of wearing our green shirt based on the achievements of this squad of players. Bring on the next tournament!

Patrick Nelson
Chief Executive
Irish Football Association

THE JOURNEY BEGINS...

Two 6-0 defeats in their opening three games would make most managers question their philosophy and tactics. But not Kenny Shiels.

Right from the off, following his appointment in May 2019, the Northern Ireland senior women's team manager encouraged a more expansive style of play in his squad, playing out from the back and building attacks through the midfield engine room.

And by the end of that year, despite those early setbacks, the senior women's team were well placed to make waves in their Women's Euro 2020 qualifying group (the tournament was later switched to 2021 due to the Covid pandemic).

His team were heavily defeated in Shiels' first competitive match in charge - by top seeds Norway (6-0) in their opening UEFA Women's Euro qualifier in August - but they stuck to their guns and days later produced a great performance in Wales to earn a 2-2 draw.

Striker Simone Magill opened the scoring against the Welsh with a header, while defender Ashley Hutton headed in a last-minute equaliser, which would prove decisive in the final shake-up in Qualifying Group C.

Another 6-0 defeat to Norway followed in November, however they again deservedly earned a draw against Wales, second seeds in Group C, a few days later.

And that 0-0 draw in Belfast set them up nicely for qualifiers home and away against Belarus and Faroe Islands in 2020.

Also during 2019 the senior women's team welcomed a second centurion into their ranks.

The previous year Julie Nelson became the first female player in Northern Ireland to earn 100 caps and she was followed by her defensive partner Ashley Hutton as she reached the 100-cap milestone.

Ashley earned her 100th cap in Wales and was subsequently presented with a UEFA medal at the home game against the Welsh.

Norway, the top seeds in Group C, showed a ruthless streak as they ran out 6-0 winners against Shiels' team at Seaview in August 2019.

The Norwegians produced some mesmerising football at times, however Northern Ireland did not help their cause with costly errors.

It was always going to be tough for Shiels' side, who were up against a squad featuring players who ply their trade with the likes of Barcelona, PSG, Chelsea and Wolfsburg, however they gave a good account of themselves despite the final scoreline.

Barcelona Femini player Caroline Graham Hansen, who grabbed a hat-trick, produced an excellent individual performance on the Shore Road. Guro Reiten (two) and substitute Amalie Eikeland got the other goals.

The bulk of Martin Sjögren's squad were at the Women's World Cup in France earlier that summer where they reached the quarter-finals — and their class was evident for much of the game.

In September the girls in green and white travelled to Newport to take on the Welsh at Rodney Parade.

Magill opened the scoring on 11 minutes before Wales captain Angharad James equalised 11 minutes after that.

Welsh striker Kayleigh Green put the hosts ahead on 69 minutes, however Hutton popped up to head the ball home four minutes into added time to level the scores at 2-2.

The Northern Ireland starting line-up for that game included two players who would subsequently not be in Shiels' plans as the campaign unfolded – experienced goalkeeper Emma Higgins and midfielder Freya Holdaway, who had to retire from football in 2020 after suffering a series of concussions.

And on the subs bench was another player who was soon out of the

picture, Kerry Montgomery. However, all of them could still say they played a part in the march to the Euros.

In November the Norwegians turned on the style again to defeat Northern Ireland 6-0 in Stavanger.

Lisa-Marie Utland opened the scoring after just three minutes and was on the scoresheet again nine minutes later.

Northern Ireland keeper Becky Flaherty produced a string of fine saves to keep Norway at bay during the rest of the first half, however they fell further behind on 51 minutes when Caroline Graham Hansen played in Guro Reiten and she made no mistake.

Three more goals followed. They were scored by Ingrid Syrstad Engen and Graham Hansen (two).

A few days later Northern Ireland produced a solid display in their second Group C encounter with Wales.

Some sterling defensive work, a couple of great saves from keeper Becky Flaherty and some positive attacking play saw them deservedly seal a point with a 0-0 draw in the Qualifying Group C clash at Seaview Stadium.

There was a delay to the game early on while Flaherty, making her home debut, received treatment for a nose injury following a collision with Welsh forward Kayleigh Green.

However, she dusted herself down and produced enough heroics between the sticks to pick up the player of the match award. Her best stop was from a low James drive.

It was not all one-way traffic. Wales did have the bulk of the chances, however Magill, Rachel Furness and Lauren Wade all had decent efforts on goal.

UEFA WOMEN'S EUROPEAN CHAMPIONSHIP
QUALIFIER (GROUP C)

NORTHERN IRELAND 0
NORWAY 6

REITEN (4'), HANSEN (16', 63', 72'), EIKELAND (82', 90')

FRIDAY 30 AUGUST 2019
SEAVIEW, BELFAST
KICK-OFF 19:45

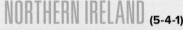

NORTHERN IRELAND (5-4-1)

J. Burns, R. Newborough, S. McFadden (captain)
(K. Montgomery 69'), J. Nelson, A. Hutton,
D. Vance (M. Callaghan 68'), R. McKenna
(L. Wade 68'), F. Holdaway, R. Furness,
C. McCarron, S. Magill

Subs not used B. Flaherty (GK), E. Higgins (GK),
Y. White, M. Bell, N. Johnson, R. Holloway

Booked S. McFadden (51')

NORWAY (4-4-2)

C. Fiskerstrand, I. Wold, M. Mjelde,
M. Thorisdottir, K. Minde, K. Saevik, V. Boe Risa,
I. Engen (A. Eikeland 71'), G. Reiten (E. Thorsnes
83'), C. Hansen, L. Karlseng Utland (F. Maanum
71').

Subs not used O. Bogstad (GK), I. Hjelmseth
(GK), T. Hansen, E. Nautnes, K. Leine, S. Hansen

Referee V. Kovarova (Czech Republic)

UEFA WOMEN'S EUROPEAN CHAMPIONSHIP
QUALIFIER (GROUP C)

WALES 2
A. JAMES (22'), K. GREEN (69')

NORTHERN IRELAND 2
S. MAGILL (11'), A. HUTTON (90')

TUESDAY 3 SEPTEMBER 2019
RODNEY PARADE, NEWPORT
KICK-OFF 19:05

PICTURES COURTESY OF FOOTBALL ASSOCIATION OF WALES

PICTURES COURTESY OF FOOTBALL ASSOCIATION OF WALES

WALES (4-4-2)

L. O'Sullivan, L. Dykes, R. Roberts, S. Ingle,
G. Evans, N .Harding, A. James, H. Ladd,
E. Hughes, E. Jones (M. Wynne 66'), K. Green

Subs not used O. Clarke (GK), C. Skinner (GK),
C. Jones, A. Fibley, J. Green, C. Estcourt,
K. Nolan, E. Powell, L. Woodham, H. Ward

Booked G. Evans (86')

NORTHERN IRELAND (5-4-1)

E. Higgins, R. Newborough (C. McCarron 88'),
A. Hutton (captain), S. McFadden, J. Nelson,
D. Vance, F. Holdaway (R. McKenna 57'), L. Wade,
R. Furness, M. Bell (M. Callaghan 60'), S. Magill

Subs not used L. Perry (GK), T. Finnegan,
R. McKenna, K. Burrows, C. Howe

Booked L. Wade (62'), R. Newborough (76'),
S. McFadden (84'), M. Bell (90+4')

Referee A. Acevedo (Spain)

PICTURES COURTESY OF FOOTBALL ASSOCIATION OF WALES

UEFA WOMEN'S EUROPEAN CHAMPIONSHIP
QUALIFIER (GROUP C)

NORWAY 6
L. KARLSENG UTLAND (3',12'), G. REITEN (51'),
I. ENGEN (53'), C. HANSEN (69',90+2')

NORTHERN IRELAND 0

FRIDAY 8 NOVEMBER 2019
SR-BANK ARENA, STAVANGER
KICK-OFF 17:00

PICTURES COURTESY OF NORWEGIAN FOOTBALL FEDERATION

NORWAY **(4-2-3-1)**

C. Fiskerstrand, S. Skinnes Hansen, M. Mjelde,
I. Engen, I. Wold, V. Boe Risa (R. Nygard 77'),
F. Maanum, K. Saevik (A. Eikeland 67'),
C. Hansen, G. Reiten, L. Karlseng Utland
(E.Thorsnes 67')

Subs not used A. Mikalsen (GK), T. Hansen,
K. Leine, S. Hoveland, V. Hasund, T. Asland,
C. Kvamme, E. Terland

NORTHERN IRELAND **(4-3-3)**

B. Flaherty, R. Newborough, A. Hutton,
J. Nelson, D. Vance, S. McFadden (captain)
(M. Callaghan 56'), C. McCarron, R. Furness
(S. Kelly 84'), M. Bell, C. McGuinness
(E. McMaster 77'), L. Wade

Subs not used L. Perry (GK), T. Finnegan,
R. McKenna, K. Burrows, C. Howe

Referee M. Ozcigdem (Turkey)

PICTURES COURTESY OF NORWEGIAN FOOTBALL FEDERATION

UEFA WOMEN'S EUROPEAN CHAMPIONSHIP
QUALIFIER (GROUP C)

NORTHERN IRELAND 0
WALES 0

TUESDAY 12 NOVEMBER 2019
SEAVIEW, BELFAST
KICK-OFF 19:45

NORTHERN IRELAND (4-4-2)

B. Flaherty, R. Newborough (R. McKenna 58'),
J. Nelson, A. Hutton, D. Vance, C. McCarron,
R. Furness, S. McFadden (captain) (M. Callaghan
80'), M. Bell, S. Magill, L. Wade

Subs not used L. Perry (GK), T. Finnegan,
K. Burrows, C. Howe, S. Kelly, Y. White,
N. Caldwell

Booked C. McCarron (79'), R. Furness (90+1')

WALES (4-4-2)

L. O'Sullivan, L. Dykes, R. Roberts, H. Ladd,
E. Hughes (G. Evans 55'), M. Wynne, S. Ingle,
J. Green, R. Rowe, K. Green (H. Ward 83'),
A. James

Subs not used O. Clarke (GK), C. Skinner (GK),
C. Jones, G. Walter, K. Nolan, M. Francis-Jones,
N. Lawrence

Booked H. Ladd (45')

Referee K. Wacker (Germany)

2020
ON THE MARCH TOWARDS A PLAY-OFF

The Northern Ireland senior women's team had a remarkable year in 2020 as they qualified for a play-off for a major tournament for the first time in the team's short history.

Kenny Shiels' side were well placed to make waves in their Women's Euro qualifying group at the start of the year – and they did that with aplomb.

Shiels introduced a more expansive style of play when he took over as senior women's manager in May 2019 and it eventually paid dividends.

They entered the new year sitting on two points following two draws against Wales, and two defeats to top seeds Norway, in their opening set of qualifiers in 2019.

But by the end of 2020 they had secured a further 12 points in Qualifying Group C to keep their Euros dream very much alive.

The away match against Belarus in Group C was scheduled for 14 April with the return fixture in Belfast on 5 June. Northern Ireland were also due to face Faroe Islands at home on 9 June before heading to the Faroes for their final group game on 18 September.

However, the coronavirus pandemic led to the postponement of the spring/summer qualifiers until the autumn.

And in April the UEFA Executive Committee confirmed the UEFA Women's Euro 2021 final tournament, which had also been postponed, would now be played in England from 6 to 31 July 2022 instead.

In March 2020 the senior women began their preparations for the qualifiers by competing at the Pinatar Cup in Spain – and the squad's performances once again showed they were making steady progress.

They lost to Iceland (1-0), Ukraine (4-0) and Scotland (2-1), countries who were ranked much higher than them, but the manager was happy with the level of performance at the tournament.

Going in to the final four qualifiers of the campaign the girls in green and white knew that four wins would guarantee a play-off, but it appeared to be a tall order given that the team had not won a competitive fixture for five years.

The 2-2 away draw and 0-0 home draw against Wales the previous year meant Northern Ireland would have a better head-to-head record - thanks to those away goals - if the two countries were neck and neck going in to the final group fixtures.

Step one for Northern Ireland was an away qualifier against Faroe Islands, which went ahead as scheduled in mid-September.

And the senior women lived up to their favourites tag as they comfortably ran out 6-0 winners in Torshavn.

It was a fourth seeds (NIR) v fifth seeds (FRO) clash in Qualifying Group C. Lauren Wade and Simone Magill both helped themselves to doubles, while Rachel Furness and Kirsty McGuinness also got on the scoresheet.

The senior players, who had followed a strict training regime delivered remotely by Shiels and his backroom staff throughout the Covid-19 pandemic, were well prepared for the game – and they were three up within half an hour as they dominated the play.

Captain Sarah McFadden and Nadene Caldwell, back in the side after a lengthy sojourn, both had strikes at goal before fellow midfielder Furness, who had earlier hit the woodwork, opened the scoring with a left foot thunderbolt on 19 minutes.

Then striker Magill doubled the lead with a tidy finish just five minutes later. Winger Wade hit the woodwork with a rasping drive and Magill was on hand to steer in the rebound.

Shortly after that Wade got in on the act, cutting in from the right to smash the ball into the bottom corner, making it 3-0 to Northern Ireland in the 27th minute.

The prolific McGuinness, playing her first match for Northern Ireland in over two years, added the fourth 11 minutes later with another neat effort. Magill slipped the ball to her inside the area and she clipped it into the net.

Northern Ireland extended their lead on 56 minutes. McCarron floated in a free-kick which was headed on by Furness to Wade and she provided the finish.

Magill grabbed her second of the game, and Northern Ireland's sixth, on 90 minutes. McCarron delivered the ball towards goal and the striker pounced to head it into the net.

Like McGuinness and Caldwell, Caragh Milligan returned to the fold for the Faroes game after a lengthy sojourn, while fellow substitute Joely Andrews made her senior debut.

The senior women then made it back-to-back wins thanks to a 1-0 victory away to Belarus in October.

Shiels' side had to play the majority of the match with 10 players after keeper Jackie Burns saw red - but it was swiftly followed by a moment of magic from Rachel Furness who netted the only goal of the game to claim a precious three points in Minsk.

Furness's goal – a bullet header – arrived three minutes before the break and could not have come at a better time for Northern Ireland who had to readjust on 27 minutes when Burns received her marching orders for a foul on Anastasija-Grazyna Shcherbachenia.

On came replacement stopper Becky Flaherty with goal threat Kirsty McGuinness making way and it looked like it could have been a long night for Shiels' side. But up stepped Furness who rose above the home defence to head home Demi Vance's pinpoint corner.

WOMEN'S EURO PLAY-OFF IS SECURED

The Northern Ireland senior women's team secured a Women's Euro 2022 play-off with two excellent home victories – against Belarus and Faroe Islands.

Following their away wins against the Faroes and Belarus in September and October respectively, a 3-2 victory over Belarus at Seaview in late November was the penultimate step towards a play-off, while the glory game against the Faroese arrived just days later.

A slightly nervous Northern Ireland had to dig deep at times against Belarus in Belfast but goals from Kirsty McGuinness and player of the match Rachel Furness (penalty) plus an own goal by the Belarus keeper were enough to secure the victory.

Kenny Shiels' side came flying out of the blocks and opened the scoring after just two minutes.

Kirsty McGuinness played in Emily Wilson but her shot was pushed away by advancing Belarus keeper Natalia Vaskabovich, however McGuinness met the rebound and rifled the ball home. It was a superb finish.

In the 16th minute Belarus grabbed an equaliser. Anastasiya Novikava played the ball forward towards Anastasija-Grazyna Shcherbachenia. Flaherty raced off her line but the striker got to

the ball first and drove the ball home from 20 yards.

The girls in green and white took the lead again in the 61st minute via the penalty spot. Furness was hauled down as Demi Vance delivered a free-kick into the area and the ref quickly pointed to the spot. Furness dusted herself down before stepping up to coolly blast the penalty into the corner of the net.

Belarus levelled on 67 minutes. Hanna Pilipenka fed Belarus captain Shcherbachenia and she slotted home her second of the night.

McGuinness conjured up the winner just three minutes later. She advanced down the left before unleashing a fierce drive which rebounded off the post but hit Vaskabovich's back and flew into the net to make it 3-2.

At the start of December the Euros dream was kept on course following a superb victory over Faroe Islands.

Despite an early setback Shiels' side dominated the game at Seaview and ran out comfortable winners on a 5-1 scoreline. Sisters Kirsty and Caitlin McGuinness both got on the scoresheet along with Chloe McCarron, while Rachel Furness grabbed a double.

The historic win meant Northern Ireland were guaranteed a play-off for a place at UEFA Women's Euro 2022 after finishing second in Qualifying Group C, pipping the Welsh thanks to their head-to-record against them.

The Faroese took the lead on four minutes. Kara Djurhuus played a clever ball to Jensa Torolvsdottir and she applied the finish.

Northern Ireland were level within two minutes. McCarron floated the ball towards goal and it was punched away by the Faroes keeper but Furness was on hand to bravely head the loose ball home.

Shiels' charges took the lead through a sublime Kirsty McGuinness strike. The striker collected a Lauren Wade pass close to the edge of the area before cutting inside and curling the ball superbly into the top corner.

Their third goal was another absolute peach. On 55 minutes Wade jinked inside down the right and slipped the ball to McCarron just outside the area. The midfielder took a touch and then unleashed an unstoppable strike into the top corner.

History was made when Caitlin McGuinness came on as a substitute in the 64th minute, replacing Emily Wilson. Caitlin and older sibling Kirsty became the first pair of sisters to feature for the Northern Ireland senior women's team in the same match.

Northern Ireland got their fourth in the 77th minute. A McCarron delivery from a corner was headed on by Julie Nelson and Caitlin McGuinness nipped in to sweep the ball into the net.

Goal number five came in the 87th minute. Kirsty McGuinness pinged a corner to the back post where Furness arrived right on cue to clip the ball home from close range off the knee of a Faroes defender for her second of the night. It was her 31st goal for Northern Ireland.

The win over the Faroese meant Northern Ireland took their place in the play-offs, the draw for which was due to be made in March 2021 after all qualifiers had been completed. The play-offs, played over two legs, were scheduled to be staged in April 2021.

PINATAR CUP

PINATAR CUP

ICELAND 1
D. BRYNJARSDOTTIR 24'

NORTHERN IRELAND 0

**WEDNESDAY 4 MARCH 2020
PINATAR FOOTBALL CENTRE,
SAN PEDRO DEL PINATAR, SPAIN
KICK-OFF 14:00**

ICELAND (4-1-4-1)

C. Runarsdottir, G. Jonsdottir, I. Siguroardottir,
G. Viggosdottir, S. Gunnarsdottir (N. Anasi 46'),
H. Eiriksdottir (S. Jessen 66'), D. Brynjarsdottir
(S. Garoarsdottir 46'), R. Honnudottir (A. Albertsdottir
66'), F. Frioriksdottir (S. Guomundsdottir 66'), E. Jensen
(H. Antonsdottir 85')

Subs not used I. Valgeirsdottir (GK), S. Siguroardottir
(GK), G. Arnadottir, A. Petursdottir, B. Agustsdottir,
E. Vioarsdottir

Booked H. Ladd (45')

NORTHERN IRELAND (4-3-3)

J. Burns, R. Newborough (R. McKenna 57'), K. Burrows,
J. Nelson, D. Vance, S. McFadden, R. Furness,
M. Callaghan (captain) (D. Maxwell 74'), M. Bell
(C. Howe 85'), S. Magill (C. McGuinness 86'), L. Wade
(E. McMaster 75')

Subs not used L. Woods (GK), C. McCarron,
T. Finnegan, A. Hutton

Referee Z. Valentova (Slovakia)

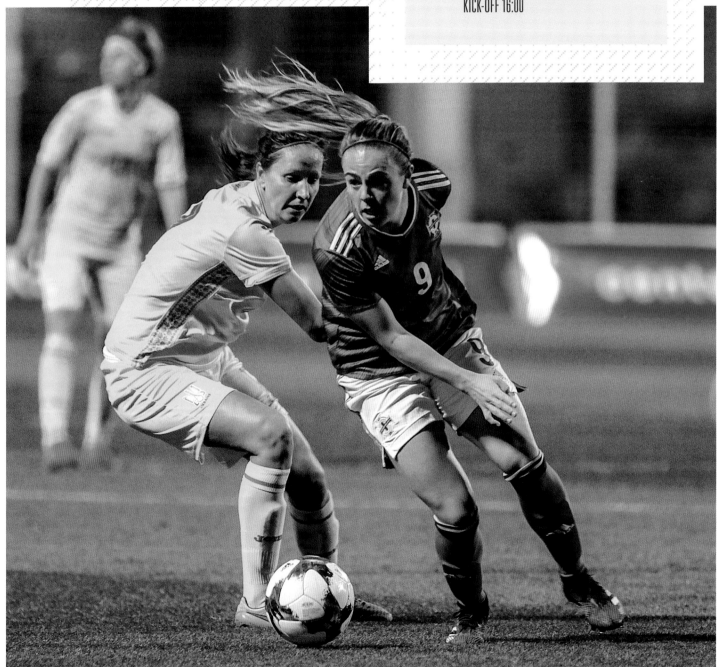

PINATAR CUP

UKRAINE 4
N. KOZLOVA (18'), D. APANASHCHENKO (33',37'), O. OVDIYCHUK (39')

NORTHERN IRELAND 0

SATURDAY 7 MARCH 2020
PINATAR FOOTBALL CENTRE,
SAN PEDRO DEL PINATAR, SPAIN
KICK-OFF 16:00

UKRAINE (4-3-3)

I. Sanina (D. Bondarchuk 74'), I. Podolska, L. Shmatko, O. Basanska (Y. Derkach 73'), N. Pantsulaia (T. Kitayeva 66'), N. Kozlova, A. Filenko, T. Khimich (N. Kunina 66'), O. Ovdiychuk (V. Andrukhiv 46'), Y. Kalinina (A. Petryk 46'), D. Apanashchenko

Subs not used K. Samson (GK), T. Romanenko, V. Tarakanova

Booked N. Pantsulaia (52'), O. Basanska (63')

NORTHERN IRELAND (4-5-1)

J. Burns, T. Finnegan (J. Nelson 46'), D. Maxwell (L. Wade 71'), A. Hutton, D. Vance, R. McKenna (M. Bell 46'), M. Callaghan (captain) (C. McCarron 71'), S. Magill, C. Howe (S. McFadden 46'), E. McMaster, C. McGuinness (R. Furness 46')

Subs not used L. Woods (GK), R. Newborough, K. Burrows

Booked D. Vance (76').

Referee P. Pavlikova (Slovakia)

SCOTLAND 2
E. CUTHBERT (35'), A. GRANT (38')

NORTHERN IRELAND 1
R. FURNESS (5')

TUESDAY 10 MARCH 2020
PINATAR FOOTBALL CENTRE,
SAN PEDRO DEL PINATAR, SPAIN
KICK-OFF 19:30

SCOTLAND (4-2-3-1)

S. Lynn, R. Boyle, S. Howard, R. Corsie,
N. Docherty, C. Murray (C. Weir 65'), L. Graham
(L. Crichton 66'), L. Arnot (A. Muir 84'), E. Cuthbert
(E. Mukandi 71'), A. Grant (H. Lauder 77'),
M. Thomas (J. Ross 85').

Subs not used L. Gibson (GK), H. Godfrey,
S. Kerr, J. Fife

Booked C. Murray (24')

NORTHERN IRELAND (4-2-3-1)

J. Burns, E. McMaster (R. Newborough 61'),
A. Hutton (T. Finnegan 80'), J. Nelson, D. Vance,
S. McFadden (captain), C. McCarron, R. McKenna
(M. Bell 46'), R. Furness, L. Wade (M. Callaghan
70'), S. Magill (C. McGuinness 80')

Subs not used L Woods (GK), K Burrows,
D Maxwell, C Howe

Booked S. McFadden (12'), D. Vance (53')

Referee P. Pavlikova (Slovakia)

UEFA WOMEN'S EUROPEAN CHAMPIONSHIP
QUALIFIER (GROUP C)

FAROE ISLANDS 0
NORTHERN IRELAND 6

R. FURNESS (19'), S. MAGILL (24',90'),
L. WADE (27',56'), K. McGUINNESS (38')

FRIDAY 18 SEPTEMBER 2020
TORSVOLLUR, TORSHAVN
KICK-OFF 17:00

FAROE ISLANDS (4-2-3-1)

E. Mikkelsen, S. Svarvadal, B. Ryan, J. Langgaard,
A. Johannesen, K. Djurhuus (L. Lisberg 83'),
E. Vang, E. A. Lakjuni (S. Lamhauge 66'),
H. Sevdal, J. Mortensen, M. Lindholm
(J. Torolvsdottir 66')

Subs not used O. Joensen (GK), O. Olsen (GK),
M. Jarnskor, U. Hvidbro, S. Mittfoss,
M. Rasmusdottir

NORTHERN IRELAND (4-4-2)

J. Burns, A. Hutton, J. Nelson, S. McFadden
(captain) (S. Kelly 65'), D. Vance, L. Wade
(C. Hamilton 78'), R. Furness, N. Caldwell
(J. Andrews 73'), C. McCarron, K. McGuinness,
S. Magill

Subs not used L. Perry (GK), R. McKenna,
R. Newborough, K. Beattie, A. Magee,
T. Finnegan

Referee G. Pirratore (Italy)

UEFA WOMEN'S EUROPEAN CHAMPIONSHIP
QUALIFIER (GROUP C)

BELARUS 0
NORTHERN IRELAND 1

R. FURNESS (42')

TUESDAY 27 OCTOBER 2020
STADYEN DYNAMA, MINSK
KICK-OFF 16:00

BELARUS (4-3-3)

E. Miklashevich, V. Kazakevich (T. Krasnova 85'),
A. Novikova, A. Kozyupa, Y. Slesarchik,
A. Kharlanova (A. Pobegaylo 59', D. Stezhko 88'),
A. Linnik, A. Pilipenko, K. Alkhovik,
A. Shcherbachenya (A. Shlapakova 84'),
A. Shuppo

Subs not used M. Svidunovich (GK),
E. Kovalchuk (GK), A. Sas, E. Dudko,
V. Nikolaenko, V. Bogdan, V. Karachun,
K. Kubichnaya

Booked A. Pilipenko (67')

NORTHERN IRELAND (4-5-1)

J. Burns, J. Nelson, A. Hutton (A. Magee 46'),
S. McFadden (captain), D. Vance, L. Wade
(C. McGuinness 90+2'), S. Magill, R. Furness,
C. McCarron, N. Caldwell (M. Callaghan 57'),
K. McGuinness (B. Flaherty 29')

Subs not used L. Perry (GK), S. Kelly, J. Andrews,
K. Burrows, N. Johnson, D. Maxwell

Sent Off J. Burns (27')

Booked S. McFadden (31')

Referee Z. Gonzalez (Spain)

UEFA WOMEN'S EUROPEAN CHAMPIONSHIP
QUALIFIER (GROUP C)

NORTHERN IRELAND 3

K. MCGUINNESS (2'), R. FURNESS (PEN 61'), N. VOSKOBOVICH (OG 70')

BELARUS 2

A. SHCHERBACHENYA (16',67')

FRIDAY 27 NOVEMBER 2020
SEAVIEW, BELFAST
KICK-OFF 19:00

NORTHERN IRELAND (4-2-3-1)

B. Flaherty, A. Hutton, C. McCarron, J. Nelson,
D. Vance (A. Magee 76'), N. Caldwell,
M. Callaghan (captain), L. Wade, R. Furness,
E. Wilson (C. Watling 86'), K. McGuinness
(S.Kelly 89')

Subs not used L. Perry (GK), C. McGuinness,
J. Andrews, D. Maxwell, K. Beattie, K. Burrows,
T. Finnegan

Booked A. Magee (90+2')'

BELARUS (4-3-3)

N. Voskobovich, V. Kazakevich, A. Novikova,
A. Kozyupa, V. Bogdan, A. Kharlanova
(K. Alkhovik 46'), A. Linnik, A. Pilipenko
(K. Kubichnaya 78'), A. Shlapakova (T. Krasnova
78'), A. Shcherbachenya, A. Shuppo

Subs not used M. Svidunovich (GK),
E. Kovalchuk (GK), A. Sas, V. Nikolaenko,
A. Pobegaylo, A. Popova, M. Surovtseva,
E. Miklashevich, V. Karachun.

Booked V. Bogdan (83')

Referee S.Domingos (Portugal)

UEFA WOMEN'S EUROPEAN CHAMPIONSHIP
QUALIFIER (GROUP C)

NORTHERN IRELAND 5

R. FURNESS (6'), K. McGUINNESS (27'), C. McCARRON (56'),
C. McGUINNESS (77'), J. LANGGAARD (OG 87')

FAROE ISLANDS 1

J. TOROLVSDOTTIR (4')

TUESDAY 1 DECEMBER 2022
SEAVIEW, BELFAST
KICK-OFF 19:00

NORTHERN IRELAND (4-4-2)

J. Burns, J. Nelson, A. Hutton (S.Kelly 64'),
S. McFadden, M.Callaghan (captain) (T. Finnegan
84'), N. Caldwell (J. Andrews 76'), C. McCarron,
R.Furness, L. Wade (D. Maxwell 84'),
K. McGuinness, E. Wilson (C. McGuinness 64')

Subs not used B. Flaherty (GK), L. Perry (GK),
K. Beattie, A. Magee, C. Watling, R. McKenna

FAROE ISLANDS (4-2-3-1)

E. Mikkelsen, S. Svarvadal, B. Ryan, J. Langgaard,
A. Johannesen, K. Djurhuus (L. Lisberg 83'),
E. Vang, E-A Lakjuni (S. Lamhauge 66'), H.
Sevdal, J. Mortensen, M. Lindholm
(J. Torolvsdottir 66')

Subs not used O. Joensen (GK), O. Olsen (GK),
M. Jarnskor, U. Hvidbro, S. Mittfoss,
M. Rasmusdottir

Booked E. Vang (90+4').

Referee H. Guteva (Bulgaria)

2021
CREATING HISTORY
WAS THE GOAL

2021 did not get off to a great start, but it was merely a blip when Northern Ireland were heavily defeated by England Women in a friendly at St George's Park in February.

Ellen White bagged a hat-trick as the Lionesses ran out 6-0 winners in blustery conditions. England's other scorers were Lucy Bronze, Rachel Daly and Ella Toone.

However, there were some fine individual performances within the Northern Ireland team, especially from young defender Abbie Magee.

The following month the draw was made for three UEFA Women's Euro 2022 play-offs and Northern Ireland were paired with Ukraine Women.

And they produced a gritty, resilient and skilful display to defeat Ukraine in the first instalment of the play-off in early April.

Goals from Rachel Furness and Simone Magill were enough to secure a famous victory at the Kolos Stadium in Kovalivka.

Participating in their first ever play-off for a major tournament, Northern Ireland started brightly and Furness pounced after just five minutes to put them one up.

Ukraine holding midfielder Tamila Khimich played a poor pass forward and the attacking midfielder nipped in to steer the ball past Ukraine keeper Iryna Sanina. The ball hit the keeper's foot on the way into the net but Furness rightly claimed the goal.

Ukraine equalised on 22 minutes when their captain and star player Darya Apanashchenko flicked a header past Northern Ireland keeper Burns into the bottom corner.

The Northern Ireland defence stood firm as the home side pushed forward, with veterans Ashley Hutton, Julie Nelson and Sarah McFadden working

tirelessly alongside wing backs Rebecca Holloway and Rebecca McKenna.

On 57 minutes Northern Ireland took the lead again when Magill got on the end of a McFadden flick-on, forced her way past her marker and neatly clipped the ball high into the net from 10 yards. It was a lovely finish.

It was backs to the wall in the closing stages, however the girls in green and white held their nerve and held on for a deserved 2-1 victory.

In the second leg at Seaview just days later Northern Ireland Women booked their place at the Euros in 2022 with a gutsy 2-0 victory - to secure a 4-1 aggregate win.

Despite being without the talismanic Furness, who broke her tibia in the first match, and seven other injured players who would have arguably been in the squad at the very least, Shiels' side produced another excellent performance.

They were defensively sound throughout and classy goals from captain Marissa Callaghan, who replaced the injured Furness in the number 10 role, and substitute Nadene Caldwell were enough to seal the historic success.

After a first half of few chances, Northern Ireland took the lead on 55 minutes when Nelson floated a free-kick into the box towards Callaghan and the skipper flicked the ball past the advancing keeper before slipping it into the net from an extremely tight angle. It was a lovely piece of skill.

In the 87th minute Ukraine were reduced to 10 players when Natiya Pantsulaya was shown a straight red for blocking off McFadden as she was running towards the Ukrainian penalty area.

Deep into added time Caldwell sealed the win for Northern Ireland. Magill nicked the ball off a Ukraine defender and nudged it to the midfielder, who cleverly rounded the keeper and stroked the ball home.

Later that month Northern Ireland Women boss Shiels signed a two-year contract extension.

Shiels, whose coaching career had taken him to clubs across Northern Ireland as well as in England, Scotland and Thailand, was initially appointed to the role in May 2019 on a part-time basis.

He succeeded Alfie Wylie, who had been in the hot seat for well over a decade and had given debuts to several of the players in the squad that reached the Euros. Wylie in turn stepped into an elite player development role within the women's international set-up where he remained until the summer of 2022.

The fresh deal for Shiels saw him given a full-time contract with the Irish FA.

The draw for the FIFA Women's World Cup 2023 qualifiers was made in April, too.

Shiels' side were placed in European Qualifying Group D along with top seeds England, Austria, North Macedonia, Latvia and Luxembourg.

In June, prior to those qualifiers getting under way in September, the senior women's team took part in a training camp which included a friendly against Scotland Women at Seaview.

Both sides created chances in the game, however a second half penalty from Scotland substitute Caroline Weir was enough to give Stuart McLaren's team a 1-0 victory.

Also in June, centurion Julie Nelson was awarded a British Empire Medal in the Queen's Birthday Honours - for services to women's football in Northern Ireland.

The central defender from Larne made her senior debut at the age of 18 in March 2004 when she faced Portugal in the Algarve Cup tournament in Portugal. She also represented her country at underage level – at U15 and U19.

Nelson, who earned her 100th cap in a FIFA Women's World Cup qualifier against Slovakia in September 2018, said: "It's an incredible honour to be on the Queen's Birthday Honours List. It's not something I ever imagined my name would be on. It's special to be on the list and to be given an honour after so many years of hard work."

2021 SWITCH OF FOCUS AFTER PLAY-OFF GLORY

After booking a place at UEFA Women's Euro 2022 thanks to their thrilling play-off success against Ukraine, the Northern Ireland senior women's team switched their focus to World Cup qualifiers in the latter part of 2021.

Northern Ireland eased past Luxembourg in their opening FIFA Women's World Cup 2023 qualifier in September.

Kenny Shiels' side comfortably won the European Qualifying Group D match at Inver Park in Larne by four goals to nil.

It was Luxembourg's first ever fixture in a full qualifying stage for a major tournament – and they found it hard to deal with Northern Ireland's attacking prowess.

Northern Ireland created more than 30 chances and constantly put the visitors under pressure.

Captain Marissa Callaghan opened the scoring with a neat lob, while Rachel Furness increased the lead with a powerful header.

Northern Ireland went 3-0 up when Furness struck the post with a free-kick and Emily Wilson was on hand to hammer in the rebound. It was her first senior international goal.

Lauren Wade grabbed goal number four when she smashed the ball into the net after a Kerry Beattie shot was blocked.

Days later another success followed – this time against Latvia.

The senior women's team marked their return to the National Football Stadium at Windsor Park with a scintillating performance against the Latvians.

They had not played at the stadium for nine years but they looked at home when registering a 4-0 win for the second game running.

Goals from Louise McDaniel, Kirsty McGuinness, Callaghan and Furness (penalty) were enough to secure the win in front of more than 4000 fans. McGuinness was given the captain's armband for the night as she won her 50th cap for Northern Ireland.

The hosts created several chances during the 90-plus minutes, just as they did in the win over Luxembourg in their opening European Qualifying Group D fixture, and they could have scored more than four.

At the end of September plans for Northern Ireland Women to train full time in preparation for UEFA Women's Euro 2022 were presented to MLAs and Ministers at Stormont.

At a reception event entitled 'A New Dream', hosted by Ulster Unionist MLA Mike Nesbitt, representatives from across the political spectrum gathered to meet members of Kenny Shiels' squad and pledge their support for the team moving from their part-time status to train on a full-time basis from January 2022.

Northern Ireland's two Women's World Cup qualifiers in October were a completely different proposition from the games in September. They faced England, the top seeds in the group, at Wembley and then second seeds Austria at Seaview a few days later.

Northern Ireland battled bravely against England at Wembley. A backs to the wall performance saw them keep the Lionesses at bay for more than an hour, however a hat-trick from substitute Beth Mead and a goal from

another substitute, Bethany England, gave the hosts a deserved 4-0 win.

They showed plenty of heart, courage and commitment throughout, however England's superior fitness and power told in the end.

Just over 23,000 fans, including a 400-plus contingent of the Green and White Army, watched England cruise to victory – eventually.

Arguably Shiels' team were battling it out with Austria for second place in the group, which would have triggered a series of play-off matches that could have resulted in qualification for the World Cup finals in Australia and New Zealand in 2023.

In the first of their battles with the Austrians, which came just days after the visit to Wembley, they produced a superb performance to draw 2-2 in Belfast.

And it could have been even better. Shiels' side were leading 2-1 after 90 minutes but the Austrians scored deep into added time to secure a point.

Northern Ireland, who had Chloe McCarron, Caragh Hamilton, Nadene Caldwell and Laura Rafferty pulled from the squad hours before kick-off due to Covid protocols, put in an unbelievable shift in front of 2,350 spectators at Seaview.

Austria were the better team in the first half and went in 1-0 up at the break through a Barbara Dunst strike. However, the home side were full of energy in the second period and deservedly went ahead thanks to cracking goals from Lauren Wade and Demi Vance.

But the visitors piled on the pressure towards the end and grabbed the leveller.

Two minutes into added time Austria captain Carina Wenninger launched the ball into the area and substitute Stefanie Enzinger was on hand to head the ball over Northern Ireland keeper Jackie Burns into the net. It was a real sucker punch.

Off the pitch in October the draw for the group stages at UEFA Women's Euro 2022 took place.

The draw was staged in Manchester on 28 October. It was originally set for 6 November 2020 but had been postponed due to the Covid-19 pandemic.

And it threw up familiar opponents for Northern Ireland. Both England and Austria, whom they had met in World Cup qualifiers earlier that month, were drawn in Group A along with Shiels' team.

The other opponents in the group would be Norway, whom the girls in green and white had faced during their successful Women's Euro qualification campaign.

In terms of venues for the Group A encounters, the draw saw Northern Ireland being located at St Mary's Stadium in Southampton, home of Southampton FC, for all three of their group games.

After the buzz surrounding the Euros draw, it was back to porridge with two World Cup qualifiers in November.

With goal difference potentially being a key factor in their group, Northern Ireland went on a scoring spree. In two clashes against North Macedonia they notched 20 goals without reply.

The senior women's team were relentless in the first instalment of their World Cup qualifiers double header against the Macedonians.

Kenny Shiels' side were simply superb as they claimed another three points with a record 11-0 victory in Skopje.

Four goals from Simone Magill, a hat-trick from Furness and goals from Rebecca McKenna, Wade, Kirsty McGuinness and Rebecca Holloway secured the sensational win.

It was the Northern Ireland senior women's team's biggest ever victory home or away – and Furness's hat-trick meant she equalled David Healy's goalscoring record for Northern Ireland on bringing her tally to 36 goals for her country.

Shiels' team completely dominated proceedings at the Football Federation of North Macedonia Training Centre.

In the match McKenna and Holloway grabbed their first senior international goals, while Rachel McLaren made her senior debut after replacing Crusaders Strikers team-mate Julie Nelson at half-time.

Northern Ireland were in cruise control once again when the Macedonians visited Seaview a few days later.

In the second game of the WWCQ double header they rattled nine goals past North Macedonia in front of 2,600 fans in north Belfast.

Kirsty McGuinness grabbed a hat-trick, Furness notched a record-breaking double, Holloway also scored two and Magill and Kerry Beattie were on target as well in the emphatic win. Beattie's goal was her first at senior international level.

Furness's brace saw her take her goalscoring tally to 38, a new record for a Northern Ireland player at senior international level.

And her exploits for Northern Ireland were recognised when the Liverpool Ladies midfielder was named as the 2021 BBC Northern Ireland Sports Personality of the Year.

Furness was presented with the BBC award by Liverpool FC manager Jurgen Klopp at the Merseyside club's training ground. He congratulated her and the Northern Ireland team on their achievements in 2021 and wished them success for UEFA Women's Euro 2022 in England.

INTERNATIONAL FRIENDLY

ENGLAND 6
E. WHITE (18',23',49'), L. BRONZE (29'),
WR. DALY (67'), E. TOONE (PEN 75')

NORTHERN IRELAND 0

TUESDAY 23 FEBRUARY 2021
ST GEORGE'S PARK, BURTON UPON TRENT
KICK-OFF 12:30

ENGLAND **(4-2-3-1)**

E. Roebuck (S. MacIver 61'), L. Bronze, S. Houghton, L. Williamson (L. Wubben-Moy 75'), A. Greenwood, J. Scott, G. Stanway, R. Daly (E. Salmon 84'), J. Nobbs (E. Toone 46'), L. Hemp (C. Kelly 61'), E. White (B. England 76')

Subs not used H. Hampton (GK), M. Turner, B. Mead

NORTHERN IRELAND **(4-4-2)**

B. Flaherty, A. Magee, J. Nelson, S. McFadden (S. Kelly 84'), R. Holloway (T. Finnegan 83'), L. Wade (L. McDaniel 73'), C. McCarron (R. McKenna 57'), N. Caldwell (K. Burrows 84'), M. Callaghan (captain) (C. Watling 58'), R. Furness, S. Magill

Subs not used M. Harvey-Clifford (GK), E. Haughey, C. Howe, E. Wilson, A. Hutton

Booked R. McKenna (90+4').

Referee L. Watson (Scotland).

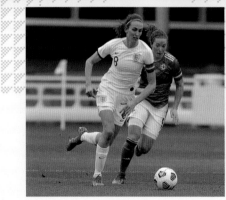

UKRAINE
WOMEN

UEFA WOMEN'S EUROPEAN CHAMPIONSHIP
PLAY-OFF (FIRST LEG)

UKRAINE 1
D.APANASHCHENKO (22')

NORTHERN IRELAND 2
R. FURNESS (5'), S. MAGILL (57')

FRIDAY 9 APRIL 2021
STADION KOLOS, KOVALIVKA
KICK-OFF 17:00

UKRAINE (4-2-3-1)

I. Sanina, A. Filenko, D. Kravets, L. Shmatko, O. Basanska (A. Petryk 81'), I. Andrushchak (N. Pantsulaia 46'), T. Khimich, O. Ovdiychuk, D. Apanashchenko (V. Andrukhiv 86'), N. Kozlova (Y. Kalinina 86'), R. Kravchuk (N. Kunina 61')

Subs not used K. Samson (GK), D. Bondarchuk (GK), O. Boychenko, A. Voronina, H. Voronina, I. Podolska, Y. Malakhova

Booked R. Kravchuk (49'), N. Pantsulaia (64'), T. Khimich (83')

NORTHERN IRELAND (3-4-2-1)

J. Burns, J. Nelson, A. Hutton, S. McFadden (L. Rafferty 79'), R. McKenna, N. Caldwell (C. Watling 79'), R. Holloway, M. Callaghan (captain), R. Furness (C. McCarron 32'), S. Magill, K. McGuinness (S. Kelly 90+4')

Subs not used B. Flaherty (GK), E. Wilson, L. McDaniel, T. Finnegan, K. Beattie, D. Maxwell, E. McMaster

Booked S. McFadden (9")

Referee R. Hussein (Germany)

UEFA WOMEN'S EUROPEAN CHAMPIONSHIP
PLAY-OFF (SECOND LEG)

NORTHERN IRELAND 2
M. CALLAGHAN (56'), N. CALDWELL (90+6')

UKRAINE 0

NORTHERN IRELAND
WON 4-1 ON AGGREGATE

TUESDAY 13 APRIL 2021
SEAVIEW, BELFAST
KICK-OFF 19:45

NORTHERN IRELAND (4-4-2)

J. Burns, R. McKenna, J. Nelson, A. Hutton,
R. Holloway, C. McCarron, L. Rafferty, S. McFadden
(T. Finnegan 90+5'), M. Callaghan (captain)
(N. Caldwell 90'), S. Magill, K. McGuinness
(S. Kelly 85')

Subs not used B. Flaherty (GK), E. Wilson,
L. McDaniel, T. Finnegan, K. Beattie, D. Maxwell,
E. McMaster

UKRAINE (4-4-2)

K. Samson, A. Filenko, D. Kravets (R. Kravchuk 69'),
L. Shmatko, O. Basanska, O. Boychenko
(Y. Malakhova 75'), N. Pantsulaia, T. Khimich,
O. Ovdiychuk, D. Apanashchenko, N. Kunina
(N. Kozlova 58')

Subs not used I. Sanina (GK), D. Bondarchuk (GK),
Y. Kalinina, I. Podolska, A. Voronina, H. Voronina,
I. Andrushchak, V. Andrukhiv

Sent off N. Pantsulaia (87')

Booked O. Basanska (29'), O. Ovdiychuk (55')

Referee J. Adamkova (Czech Republic)

INTERNATIONAL FRIENDLY

NORTHERN IRELAND 0
SCOTLAND 1

C. WEIR (78')

THURSDAY 10 JUNE 2021
SEAVIEW, BELFAST
KICK-OFF 19:00

NORTHERN IRELAND (3-4-1-2)

J. Burns, J. Nelson, S. McFadden, L. Rafferty
(E. Wilson 81') R. Mckenna, N. Caldwell (T. Finnegan
45'), C. McCarron (C. Watling 81'), R. Holloway,
M. Callaghan (captain) (K. Beattie 82'), L. Wade
(L. McDaniel 61'), K. McGuinness (S. Kelly 61')

Subs not used E. Haughey, B. Flaherty (GK),
C. Howe, F. Morgan, J. Andrews

Booked S. McFadden

SCOTLAND (4-3-3)

L. Alexander (captain), R. McLauchlan, B. Westrup
(L. Eddie 79'), S. Howard, N. Docherty, C. Murray
(L. Graham 90'), C. Arthur, L. Robertson (C. Weir 64'),
K. Hanson (L. Arnot 79'), L. Clelland (F. Brown 45'),
C. Emslie (C. Grimshaw 90')

Subs not used K. Smith, E. Cummings, R. Corsie,
E. Cuthbert, J. Fife, K. Little,

Referee C. Foster

FIFA WOMEN'S WORLD CUP 2023 QUALIFIER
(EUROPEAN GROUP D)

NORTHERN IRELAND 4
M. CALLAGHAN (16'), R. FURNESS (23'), E. WILSON (41'), L. WADE (70')

LUXEMBOURG 0

FRIDAY 17 SEPTEMBER 2021
INVER PARK, LARNE
KICK-OFF 19:00

NORTHERN IRELAND (4-2-3-1)

J. Burns, R. McKenna, J. Nelson (C. McGuinness 84'), S. McFadden (N. Caldwell 75'), R. Holloway, C. McCarron, M. Callaghan (captain) (L. McDaniel 75'), L. Wade, R. Furness (D. Vance 60'), K. McGuinness, E. Wilson (K. Beattie 60')

Subs not used B. Flaherty (GK), M. Harvey-Clifford (GK), K. Burrows, L. Rafferty, D. Maxwell, C. Hamilton, C. Watling

LUXEMBOURG (4-2-3-1)

L. Schlime, I. Albert (G. De Lemos Crespo 58'), E. Kremer (N. Raths 78'), J. Berscheid. J. De Bruyn (N. Tiberi 57'), M. Soares, L. Miller, J. Marques (A. Besch 68), E. Kocan, K. Dos Santos (K. Mendes 78), M. Garcia

Subs not used L. Krier (GK), N. Kremer (GK), A. Dervisevic, J. Becker, C. Have, H. Thill, M. Scho

Booked I. Albert (14'), J. De Bruyn (39'), K. Dos Santos (42'), E. Kremer (50'), J. Berschied (53'), N. Raths (85')

Referee E. Antoniou (Greece)

FIFA WOMEN'S WORLD CUP 2023 QUALIFIER (EUROPEAN GROUP D)

NORTHERN IRELAND 4

L. McDANIEL (48'), K. McGUINNESS (65'), M. CALLAGHAN (78'), R. FURNESS (PEN 82')

LATVIA 0

TUESDAY 21 SEPTEMBER 2021
NATIONAL FOOTBALL STADIUM
AT WINDSOR PARK, BELFAST
KICK-OFF 19:00

NORTHERN IRELAND (4-3-3)

J. Burns, L. McDaniel, L. Rafferty (K. Burrows 83'),
S. McFadden, D. Vance, C. McCarron, R. Furness
(C. Watling 84'), M. Callaghan, L. Wade (C. Hamilton
71'), K. Beattie (R. McKenna 61'), K. McGuinness
(captain) (D. Maxwell 84')

Subs not used B. Flaherty (GK),
M. Harvey-Clifford (GK), E. Wilson, N. Caldwell,
R. Holloway, C. McGuinness, J. Nelson

Booked R. Furness (19')

LATVIA (4-2-3-1)

E. Vaivode, S. Voitane (N. Brahmane 90'),
S. Gergeleziu, A. Rovane, L. Tumane (K. Girzda
90'), K. Miksone, A. Lubina (S. Garanca 90+1'),
V. Zaicikova, R. Fedotova (T. Baliceva 52'),
O. Sevcova, S. Senberga (A. Valaka 63')

Subs not used A. Sklemenova (GK),
L. Sinutkina (GK), S. Vitmore, J. Buklovska,
L. Sondore, E. Friedenfelde, K. Lodzina

Booked K. Miksone (81'), O. Sevcova (88'),
A. Lubina (90')

Referee E. Staubli (Switzerland)

FIFA WOMEN'S WORLD CUP 2023 QUALIFIER
(EUROPEAN GROUP D)

ENGLAND 4
B. MEAD (64',74',78'), B. ENGLAND (72')

NORTHERN IRELAND 0

SATURDAY 23 OCTOBER 2021
WEMBLEY STADIUM, LONDON
KICK-OFF 17:15

ENGLAND (4-3-3)

M. Earps, R. Daly (B. Mead 64'), M. Bright,
A. Greenwood (L. Staniforth 80'), D. Stokes
(K. Walsh 46'), F. Kirby (L. Wubben-Moy 80'),
L. Williamson, E. Toone, N. Parris (B. England 63'),
E. White, L. Hemp

Subs not used H. Hampton (GK), S. MacIver (GK),
A. Russo, J. Scott, G. Stanway, N. Charles, J. Carter

NORTHERN IRELAND (5-4-1)

J. Burns, R. McKenna, J. Nelson, S. McFadden,
K. Burrows (C. Watling 73'), D. Vance, C. Hamilton
(K. McGuinness 64'), C. McCarron, R. Furness
(L. McDaniel 74'), L. Wade (K. Beattie 81'),
M. Callaghan (captain) (E. Wilson 81')

Subs not used B. Flaherty (GK),
M. Harvey-Clifford (GK), L. Rafferty, J. Andrews,
N. Caldwell, R. McLaren

Booked K. Burrows (60')

Referee I. Martincic (Croatia)

FIFA WOMEN'S WORLD CUP 2023 QUALIFIER
(EUROPEAN GROUP D)

NORTHERN IRELAND 2
L. WADE (46'), D. VANCE (50')

AUSTRIA 2
B. DUNST (42'), S. ENZINGER (90+1')

TUESDAY 26 OCTOBER 2021
SEAVIEW, BELFAST
KICK-OFF 19:00

NORTHERN IRELAND (4-4-2)

J. Burns, K. Burrows, J. Nelson, S. McFadden,
D. Vance, R. McKenna, R. Furness, M. Callaghan
(captain), K. McGuinness (J. Foy 87'), K. Beattie
(E. Wilson 90+3'), L. Wade (S. Magill 79')

Subs not used B. Flaherty (GK), M. Harvey-Clifford
(GK), R. McLaren, J. Andrews, L. McDaniel,
E. McMaster, C. Watling

AUSTRIA (4-1-4-1)

M. Zinsberger, L. Wienroither, C. Wenninger,
V. Kirchberger, V. Hanshaw, S. Puntigam, B. Dunst,
S. Zadrazil, M. Hobinger (L. Feiersinger 71'),
K. Naschenweng (S. Enzinger 82')

Subs not used J. Pal (GK), V. Gritzner (GK),
K. Wienerroither, A. Schasching, M. Plattner,
M. Georgieva, C. Degen, K. Schiechtl, V. Pinther,
J. Eder

Booked C. Wenninger (49'), V. Kirchberger (71').

Referee M. Huerta (Spain).

FIFA WOMEN'S WORLD CUP 2023 QUALIFIER
(EUROPEAN GROUP D)

NORTH MACEDONIA 0
NORTHERN IRELAND 11

R. FURNESS (4', PEN 16', 68'), R. McKENNA (10'),
S. MAGILL (11', 42', 73', 90'), L. WADE (26'),
K. McGUINNESS (33'), R. HOLLOWAY (90+1')

THURSDAY 25 NOVEMBER 2021
TRAINING CENTAR PETAR
MILOSEVSKI, SKOPJE
KICK-OFF 12:00

NORTH MACEDONIA (4-2-3-1)

M. Lekoska, T. Gjorgjevska (J. Zivikj 54'),
A. Milchevska, V. Nedeva (E. Paneska 54'),
A. Boseska, A. Markovska (H. Mustafa 54'),
E. Shemsovikj, A. Salihi, K. Mileska (E. Petrovska
75'), U. Maksuti, K. Petrushevska (R. Choneva 79')

Subs not used K. Pavlovska (GK), V. Kolevska (GK),
H. Joshevska, S. Husein, S. Velkova, S. Kolarovska,
T. Jankovska

Booked T. Gjorgjevska (39'), J. Zivikj (56'),
A. Boseska (87')

NORTHERN IRELAND (4-4-2)

J. Burns, R. McKenna (C. Hamilton 77'), J. Nelson
(R. McLaren 46'), S. McFadden (K. Burrows 56'),
D. Vance, L. Wade, R. Furness (N. Caldwell 73'),
M. Callaghan (captain), (C. McCarron 46'),
R. Holloway, S. Magill, K. McGuinness

Subs not used B. Flaherty (GK),
M. Harvey-Clifford (GK), C. Watling, L. McDaniel,
K. Beattie, J. Andrews

Booked J. Nelson (45+2'), R. Holloway (67')

Referee F. Wildfeuer (Germany)

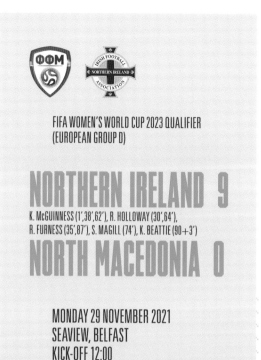

FIFA WOMEN'S WORLD CUP 2023 QUALIFIER
(EUROPEAN GROUP D)

NORTHERN IRELAND 9

K. McGUINNESS (1',38',62'), R. HOLLOWAY (30',64'),
R. FURNESS (35',87'), S. MAGILL (74'), K. BEATTIE (90+3')

NORTH MACEDONIA 0

MONDAY 29 NOVEMBER 2021
SEAVIEW, BELFAST
KICK-OFF 12:00

NORTHERN IRELAND (4-4-2)

J. Burns, R. McKenna (J. Andrews 46'), J. Nelson,
S. McFadden (C. Watling 46'), D. Vance, L. Wade,
R. Furness, M. Callaghan (captain) (L. McDaniel 65'),
R. Holloway (C. McGuinness 83'), S. Magill,
K. McGuinness (K. Beattie 70')

Subs not used B. Flaherty (GK),
M. Harvey-Clifford (GK), N. Caldwell, R. McLaren,
C. McCarron, C. Hamilton, K. Burrows

NORTH MACEDONIA (4-2-3-1)

M. Lekoska, T. Jankovska, K. Mileska,
A. Milchevska, A. Boseska, E. Petrovska,
E. Shemsovikj (A. Markovska 46'), U. Maksuti,
H. Mustafa (T. Gjorgjevska 86'), A. Salihi
(S. Husein 78'), K. Petrushevska (S. Velkova 55')

Subs not used K. Pavlovska (GK), V. Kolevska (GK),
R. Choneva, S. Kolarovska, V. Nedeva,
J. Chubrinovska, H. Joshevska, E. Paneska

Referee M. Shemesh (Israel)

2022
THE YEAR OF THE BIG ADVENTURE

The year of the big tournament began with a set of friendlies followed by FIFA Women's World Cup 2023 qualifiers followed by another friendly.

The main focus in January, however, was the full-time training programme for Northern Ireland-based players and how that would unfold in the run-up to UEFA Women's Euro 2022 in July.

February brought the players involved in the training camp and professional players with clubs in England, Scotland and elsewhere together for the first time.

Ahead of them were three friendlies at the Marbella Football Centre in Spain.

They were not fully recognised international matches – no caps were awarded to the players taking part in the games – but they certainly served a purpose in terms of boosting preparations.

First up in the Costa Del Sol was a game against Faroe Islands which Shiels' team won 3-1. Game two was against Switzerland which ended in a 2-2 draw. And the final encounter was against a strong Romania side, which ended 1-0 in the Romanians' favour.

Goals from Sam Kelly, Sarah McFadden and a beautiful strike from Chloe McCarron were the attacking highlights of a dominant display against the Faroes.

The second training match in Spain brought another positive result as Northern Ireland drew with the Swiss. Striker Simone Magill netted both goals for Shiels' side.

And they completed their 10-day camp on the Costa del Sol with a 1-0 loss to Romania.

Next up were two key FIFA Women's World Cup 2023 qualifiers (European Qualifying Group D) in April — against Austria away and then England at home.

Kenny Shiels' side never really got going against the Austrians, who won 3-1 to move three points ahead of them in European Qualifying Group D with three games in the qualifying series to go.

Goals from Austria captain Carina Wenninger, Nicole Billa and Barbara Dunst put the home side well on top before substitute Joely Andrews fired home a consolation for the visitors in front of 1,200 fans in Wiener Neustadt.

Northern Ireland started brightly but the home side some began to exert pressure in blustery and rainy conditions.

Just after the restart Austria took the lead through Wenninger. She lost her marker as a corner was delivered by Dunst and the skipper's clever back-heel volley flew past Burns into the bottom corner.

Then Austria keeper Manuela Zinsberger fumbled a free-kick from Vance and Simone Magill's close range effort was blocked.

Zinsberger stopped a goal-bound shot from Northern Ireland captain Marissa Callaghan before Austria doubled their lead in the 55th minute. Billa robbed the ball off Burns as she attempted to deal with a loose Julie Nelson back pass and the striker stroked the ball home from distance.

Two minutes later it was 3-0 to the Austrians. Laura Feiersinger fed the ball through to Dunst and she coolly slotted it past Burns.

Sarah McFadden scooped a shot wide as Northern Ireland showed some attacking verve in the final quarter.

Furness had a back post header plucked out of the air by Zinsberger as the girls in green and white showed more purpose.

Callaghan, who continued to press and probe, was unlucky to see her cross blocked after some neat footwork inside the area, and a Magill header was pushed away by Zinsberger.

Northern Ireland pulled one back through Andrews on 85 minutes. The substitute picked up a clearance from a corner and drilled it low and hard from long range through a sea of bodies into the bottom corner.

It was then back to Belfast for a meeting with group leaders England.

And unfortunately the ruthless Lionesses swept Northern Ireland aside at the National Football Stadium at Windsor Park.

Two goals apiece from Lauren Hemp and Georgia Stanway, plus another from Ella Toone, saw Sarina Wiegman's

team seal a comfortable 5-0 victory in front of a record crowd of 15,348.

It was backs to the wall for Northern Ireland for much of the 90-plus minutes as England launched attack after attack and cemented their place at the top of European Qualifying Group D.

The result, coupled with Austria's demolition of Latvia the same night, meant Northern Ireland's very slim chance of reaching a World Cup play-off had gone.

Hemp, Ellen White and Beth Mead spurned opportunities early on. Toone scooped a shot wide of the target before McFadden produced a superb block to keep out White.

Next to try her luck for the visitors was Lucy Bronze, whose rasping shot from an angle went inches past the post.

England opened the scoring on 26 minutes. Hemp played a one-two with Toone and cleverly dinked the ball over Jackie Burns from eight yards.

Julie Nelson made a couple of important interceptions as the wave of white shirts continued to flow forward and then her backline partner McFadden made another important block to keep out White.

A long ball over the top had Lauren Wade racing towards goal, however

England captain Leah Williamson snuffed out the danger, heading the ball into the arms of keeper Mary Earps.

The second half began as the first ended, with England on the attack. White fired a low shot towards goal which was gathered in by Burns.

England doubled their lead on 51 minutes. Bronze used all her power and strength to force her way past a couple of Northern Ireland defenders and play the ball across the face of goal where Toone tucked it away.

Moments later Northern Ireland had their first real chance. Joely Andrews broke forward and fed Wade, whose low shot was pushed away by Earps.

Down the other end Burns did well to dive full length to push out a cross-cum-shot from Hemp.

However, Hemp grabbed her second of the night in the 60th minute when a pass from Williamson deflected off Nelson into her path. The winger rounded Burns and stroked the ball into the net.

England grabbed goal number four in the 70th minute. This time Toone turned provider as she fed Stanway and she coolly stabbed the ball past Burns.

Hemp slipped in substitute Bethany England but Burns saved well at her feet before Stanway grabbed her second on 79 minutes, clipping the ball home.

As the clock wound down Hemp was still full of energy and Burns had to smother a low drive from her, while Toone's effort from distance was clasped by the Northern Ireland keeper and Millie Bright clipped the top of the bar with a rasping shot.

Northern Ireland's next match was a friendly against Belgium in June ahead of the Euros.

Then it was off to England for a big, big adventure – and the small matter of matches against Norway, Austria and the tournament hosts.

Those four games in June/July are documented in a special section in this book from pages 89 to 143.

And Northern Ireland's remaining competitive games of 2022 - two World Cup qualifiers - are documented in pages 144 to 147.

Northern Ireland rounded off a memorable and historic year with a fine 1-0 victory over Italy in a friendly at Seaview in mid-November.

PLAYERS ENJOY FULL-TIME TRAINING PROGRAMME

Northern Ireland's preparations for UEFA Women's Euro 2022 began in earnest in January when a six-month training programme kicked off.

The creation of the camp by the Irish FA meant players in the squad who did not play the game professionally in England, Scotland or further afield would become full-time players in the run-up to the tournament.

"We will do everything we can to prepare the squad for this fantastic occasion," said Irish FA Chief Executive Patrick Nelson at the time.

"It has been a huge undertaking to put such an operation together over the last few months. We are, of course, used to short term international training get-togethers, but never before have we run a six-month camp with the financial, operational, technical, welfare and medical support such a project demands," he pointed out.

A total of 22 Northern Ireland-based players trained under the non-residential full-time programme, which was based at Newforge Sports Complex in south Belfast.

Squad members who played professionally in England and Scotland remained with their clubs to train except if selected for games in international windows in February, April and June ahead of the tournament.

Northern Ireland senior women's team boss Kenny Shiels said: "2022 will be a pivotal year for my squad and backroom team. Having a permanent base at Newforge will help us collectively to maximise our potential in readiness for World Cup qualifiers and, of course, competing at the Euros in England."

Angela Platt, the Irish FA's Director of Women's Football, said: "Up to now many of our players have balanced studying or employment, or both, with training commitments to prepare to compete at the highest level in our sport.

"Competing with the best requires a level of commitment that makes full-time employment virtually impossible. With this programme now in place it will enable our squad to fully focus on being elite athletes and give us the best chance of success in Southampton later this year.

"To the employers, education organisations and clubs we say a big thank you for their support in releasing players from their current commitments to be part of this exciting and innovative programme."

The camp's training schedule covered every day of the week except Saturdays; Saturday was the scheduled day off for players.

Shiels had a fluid training schedule, however each week there were pitch sessions (both tactical and physical which were tailored on group and one-on-one basis and included match scenarios), individual and group strengthening and conditioning plus balanced rest and recovery sessions.

There were also performance analysis sessions along with physiotherapy, massage and cryospa treatments. And there were psychology (both individual and team) sessions, too.

During the six-month camp the players also carried out ambassador work to support Irish FA Foundation activities.

The programme also went on the road, with the players enjoying a training camp at the Marbella Football Centre in Spain, where they also played three matches.

THE FULL-TIME TRAINING SQUAD

The 22-strong full-time training squad based at Newforge Sports Complex in south Belfast from January until June featured:

Goalkeepers
Maddy Harvey-Clifford (Crusaders Strikers), Lilie Woods (Mid Ulster Ladies).

Defenders
Kelsie Burrows and Toni-Leigh Finnegan (both Cliftonville Ladies), Ashley Hutton and Abbie Magee (both Linfield Ladies), Julie Nelson and Rachel McLaren (both Crusaders Strikers).

Midfielders
Nadene Caldwell, Samantha Kelly, Joely Andrews, Chloe McCarron, Caragh Hamilton (all Glentoran Women), Marissa Callaghan and Louise McDaniel (Cliftonville Ladies), Vicky Carleton (Linfield Ladies).

Forwards
Lauren Wade and Danielle Maxwell (both Glentoran Women), Kirsty McGuinness and Caitlin McGuinness (both Cliftonville Ladies), Emily Wilson (Crusaders Strikers), Cora Chambers (Sion Swifts Ladies).

FRIENDLY/TRAINING MATCH

FAROE ISLANDS 1

L. WADE (OG 69')

NORTHERN IRELAND 3

S. KELLY (6'), S. McFADDEN (40'), C. McCARRON (45')

WEDNESDAY 16 FEBRUARY 2022
MARBELLA TRAINING CENTRE,
COSTA DEL SOL, SPAIN

FRIENDLY/TRAINING MATCH

SWITZERLAND 2

A. LEHMANN (51'), R. BACHMANN (54')

NORTHERN IRELAND 2

S. MAGILL (44', PEN 72')

SUNDAY 20 FEBRUARY 2022
MARBELLA TRAINING CENTRE,
COSTA DEL SOL, SPAIN

FRIENDLY/TRAINING MATCH

NORTHERN IRELAND 0

ROMANIA 1

C. MARCU (63')

WEDNESDAY 23 FEBRUARY 2022
MARBELLA TRAINING CENTRE,
COSTA DEL SOL, SPAIN

FIFA WOMEN'S WORLD CUP 2023 QUALIFIER
(EUROPEAN GROUP D)

AUSTRIA 3
C. WENNINGER (48'), N. BILLA (55'), B. DUNST (57')

NORTHERN IRELAND 1
J. ANDREWS (85')

FRIDAY 8 APRIL 2022
STADION WIENER NEUSTADT,
WIENER NEUSTADT
KICK-OFF 19:30

AUSTRIA (4-1-4-1)

M. Zinsberger, L. Wienroither, C. Wenninger, M. Georgieva, V. Hanshaw, S. Puntigam, K. Naschenweng (L. Makas 90'), S. Zadrazil, L. Feiersinger, B. Dunst (L. Kolb 73'), N. Billa (S. Enzinger 61').

Subs not used I. Kresche (GK), M. El Sheridf (GK), J. Eder, M. Hobinger, S. Hillebrand, M. Plattner, C. Degen, K. Schiechtl, L. Fuchs

NORTHERN IRELAND (3-4-2-1)

J. Burns, J. Nelson, S. McFadden, D. Vance, A. Magee (E. Wilson 90'), C. McCarron (J. Andrews 80'), R. Furness, R. Holloway (C. McGuinness 61'), L. Wade (M. Bell 80'), M. Callaghan (captain), S. Magill (K. McGuinness 90').

Subs not used B. Flaherty (GK), K. Burrows, N. Caldwell, T. Finnegan, R. McKenna, C. Hamilton

Referee S. Frappart (France).

FIFA WOMEN'S WORLD CUP 2023 QUALIFIER
(EUROPEAN GROUP D)

NORTHERN IRELAND 0
ENGLAND 5

L. HEMP (26',60'), E. TOONE (52'), G. STANWAY (70',79')

TUESDAY 12 APRIL 2022
NATIONAL FOOTBALL STADIUM
AT WINDSOR PARK, BELFAST
KICK-OFF 19:55

NORTHERN IRELAND (5-3-2)

J. Burns, A. Magee (C. Hamilton 82'), J. Nelson,
S. McFadden, K. Burrows (R. McKenna 76'),
D. Vance, J. Andrews (N. Caldwell 75'), R. Furness
(C. McCarron 61'), M. Callaghan (captain), S. Magill,
L. Wade (K. McGuinness 62')

Subs not used B. Flaherty (GK), M. Bell, K. Beattie,
T. Finnegan, R. Holloway, E. Wilson

Booked D. Vance (72')

ENGLAND (4-3-3)

M. Earps, L. Bronze, M. Bright, L. Williamson,
J. Carter (R. Daly 66'), G. Stanway (J. Nobbs 87'),
K. Walsh, E. Toone, B. Mead (N. Parris 71'), E. White
(B. England 65'), L. Hemp

Subs not used E. Roebuck (GK),
H. Hampton (GK), N. Charles, A. Russo, K. Zelem,
G. George, D. Stokes

Referee R. Hussein (Germany)

A DREAM COME TRUE

NORTHERN IRELAND LOSE TO RED FLAMES IN WARM-UP GAME

Northern Ireland suffered a 4-1 defeat against Belgium in their final warm-up match before the UEFA Women's Euros.

FRIENDLY INTERNATIONAL

BELGIUM 4
T. WULLAERT (24',86'), E. VAN KERKHOVEN (82'),
L. RAFFERTY (OG 90+3')

NORTHERN IRELAND 1
L. WADE (45+1')

THURSDAY 23 JUNE 2022
HERMAN VANDERPOORTEN STADION, LIER
KICK-OFF 19:00

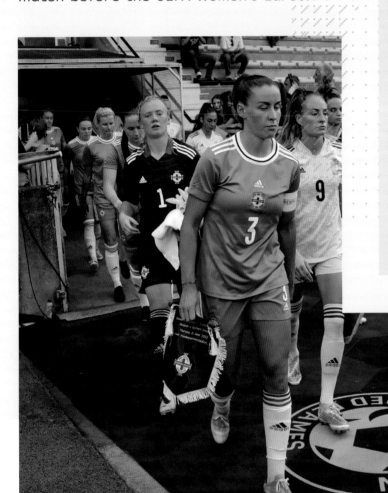

Kenny Shiels' side played the last 20 minutes of the friendly in Lier with 10 players after goalkeeper Jackie Burns was given her marching orders.

And the game stood at 1-1 until the final 10 minutes when the Red Flames piled on the pressure and scored three late goals.

Northern Ireland matched the Belgians for long spells, however the extra player proved crucial in the closing stages.

Shiels' side started brightly in humid conditions in front of just over 1000 fans.

Belgium keeper Nicky Evrard had to be on her toes to claw out a cross-cum-shot from Kirsty McGuinness.

And Lauren Wade scuffed a shot wide of the target before Abbie Magee produced a superb covering tackle to stop Belgium striker Hannah Eurlings in her tracks as she sped into the area.

Belgium took the lead in the 24th minute following a sweeping move. Laura De Neve played an excellent defence-splitting pass to set Davina Philtjens free down the left. She squared the ball to captain Tessa Wullaert who neatly tucked it into the bottom corner.

At this stage Belgium were enjoying the bulk of the possession, however Shiels' side defended stoutly.

Northern Ireland equalised a minute into added time at the end of the first half thanks to a sweet strike from Wade. Kirsty McGuinness battled for the ball on the edge of the area and it dropped to the advancing Wade who blasted it superbly past Evrard.

After the break Jackie Burns dived full length to push away a well-hit shot from midfielder Tine De Caigny and Julie Biesmans' effort was deflected out for a corner. Wullaert also flicked a header wide.

Burns was sent off in the 69th minute. The Northern Ireland keeper clattered Wullaert just outside the area as she bore down on goal and was immediately shown the red card. Becky Flaherty replaced her between the sticks.

Belgium regained the lead on 82 minutes when substitute Ella Van Kerkhoven got on the end of a Dhont cross and powerfully headed the ball home.

Minutes later it was 3-1 when captain Wullaert scored with a lovely strike from outside the area.

Van Kerkhoven got her second goal of the game as the final whistle approached. Flaherty pushed out a Wullaert header and Van Kerkhoven was on hand to poke the rebound in from two yards out.

BELGIUM (4-3-3)

N. Evrard, S. Kees (E. Dhont 46'), A. Tysiak
(F. Delacauw 85'), L. De Neve, D. Philtjens,
J. Cayman (L. Deloose 66'), J. Vanhaevermaet
(K. Missipo 78'), J. Biesmans, H. Eurlings
(D. Vanmechelen 66'), T. De Caigny
(E. Van Kerkhoven 78'), T. Wullaert

Subs not used L. Lichtfus (GK), D. Lemey (GK),
M. Minnaert, J. Janssens, S. Wijnants

NORTHERN IRELAND (3-4-3)

J. Burns, J. Nelson (L. Rafferty 46'), S. McFadden
(R. Holloway 66'), K. Burrows (A. Hutton 79'),
A. Magee, N. Caldwell, R. Furness (C. McCarron 65'),
D. Vance (captain), S. Magill, L. Wade (B. Flaherty 71'),
K. McGuinness (E. Wilson 46')

Subs not used C. McGuinness, L. McDaniel,
K. Beattie, T. Finnegan, J. Andrews

Booked L. Rafferty (90+1')

Sent Off J. Burns (69')

Referee V. Beyer (France)

ADIDAS CREATES SPECIAL KITS FOR WOMEN'S TEAM

Adidas created two new kits for the Northern Ireland senior women's team to wear at UEFA Women's Euro 2022.

The green home kit - the first Northern Ireland kit designed solely for the senior women's team - was introduced in April, while the white away kit was unveiled on the eve of the Euros.

Belgium, Germany, Spain and Sweden also donned new adidas kits at the tournament in England.

"We saw each kit as a canvas for creativity and an opportunity to capture and reimagine the DNA of each nation, connecting players and fans with a shared identity to feel a sense of belonging and confidence over the course of the tournament," said Nick Craggs, general manager of adidas Football.

"Our aim was to create kits that helped the players be the best versions of themselves," he added.

On launching the kits, adidas' international teams joined forces to work towards a bigger goal: to help end plastic waste.

The kits were created using recycled materials made with Parley Ocean Plastic and featured the latest in adidas's fabric innovations. Its sweat-wicking Aeroready technology is designed to keep players and fans cool when the heat turns up.

EUROS SQUAD IS UNVEILED

The squad to represent Northern Ireland at UEFA Women's Euro 2022 – Northern Ireland Women's first major tournament – was unveiled at the end of June.

Kenny Shiels chose a panel packed with experience and a sprinkling of youth to compete in England.

It featured two centurions in Crusaders Strikers defender Julie Nelson and Linfield Ladies defender Ashley Hutton, who had battled back to fitness from a serious knee injury to take her place in the panel.

Cliftonville Ladies midfielder Marissa Callaghan was recovering from a toe injury when the announcement was made, however she was named as the captain of the squad. And she would go on to play in all three matches at the Euros, although she did not start in the first game.

Callaghan was among a handful of players in the group who had earned between 70 and 100 caps. Liverpool Women midfielder Rachel Furness, Rangers Women defender Demi Vance, Durham Women defender Sarah McFadden and striker Simone Magill, who had just recently left Women's Super League side Everton Women, fell into that category.

And Glentoran Women midfielder Nadene Caldwell and Cliftonville Ladies forward Kirsty McGuinness were in the 50 caps-plus bracket.

Shiels also gave youth a chance. Lewes Women defender Rebecca McKenna, Cliftonville Ladies trio Kelsie Burrows, Abbie Magee and

Caitlin McGuinness, Glentoran Women midfielder Joely Andrews and Crusaders Strikers forward Emily Wilson were all aged 21 or under, while Cliftonville Ladies midfielder Louise McDaniel was 22.

The only uncapped player in the group was Wolverhampton Wanderers Women keeper Shannon Turner, who had previously represented her country at U19 level.

Forward Kerry Beattie, without a club at the time, and Cliftonville Ladies defender Toni-Leigh Finnegan, who were both in the squad for the friendly against Belgium earlier that month, did not make the cut. And nor did Southampton Women midfielder Ciara Watling.

FOLLOW @NORTHERNIRE

Finnegan was not the only player who had been part of the Belfast-based full-time training squad to miss out. The others were Crusaders Strikers defender Rachel McLaren, Crusaders Strikers goalkeeper Maddy Harvey-Clifford, Mid-Ulster Ladies goalkeeper Lilie Woods and Sion Swifts Ladies striker Cora Chambers.

And missing out through injury were Rangers Women midfielder Megan Bell, Glentoran Women midfielders Caragh Hamilton and Sam Kelly, Glentoran Women striker Danielle Maxwell and Linfield Ladies midfielder Vicky Carleton.

Other players who had been in squads during the Euro qualifiers but were not in the final shake-up included Emma Higgins, Rachel Newborough, Freya Holdaway, Kerry Montgomery, Emma McMaster, Natalie Johnson, Lauren Perry, Casey Howe and Yasmin White.

The squad was initially announced on the Irish FA website and social media channels and included an animated

video voiced by Derry Girls star and Northern Ireland fan Tara Lynne O'Neill.

The video was illustrated by Belfast-based design agency Landmark, with creative direction provided by Tim Farrell and Glenn Kennedy from the agency along with the Irish FA's digital content manager, John Gillespie. It was animated by Bristol-based animation studio Sons Of Graham.

The announcement featured across numerous broadcast and online media platforms.

It was followed by an event at the National Football Stadium at Windsor Park, attended by more than 100 guests and fans, and there was also a press conference for invited media.

The stadium event included a panel discussion featuring former Northern Ireland international Kelly Bailie, Irish FA Director of Women's Football Angela Platt, also an ex-international, and Irish FA President Conrad Kirkwood.

ENGLAND 2022

JACKIE BURNS
GOALKEEPER
READING WOMEN

 MINUTES PLAYED AT EUROS
270-PLUS

AGE 25   CAPS 44   GOALS 0

HAD JUST LEFT BK HACKEN (SWE) BEFORE
EUROS, NOW WITH READING IN WSL

BECKY FLAHERTY
GOALKEEPER
BRIGHOUSE TOWN

 MINUTES PLAYED AT EUROS
0

AGE 24   CAPS 7   GOALS 0

SHANNON TURNER
GOALKEEPER
WOLVERHAMPTON WANDERERS WOMEN

MINUTES PLAYED AT EUROS
0

AGE 24   CAPS 0   GOALS 0

JULIE NELSON
DEFENDER
CRUSADERS STRIKERS

MINUTES PLAYED AT EUROS
262

AGE 37   CAPS 130   GOALS 9

ASHLEY HUTTON
DEFENDER
LINFIELD LADIES

MINUTES PLAYED AT EUROS
3

AGE 34   CAPS 115   GOALS 9

NOW RETIRED FROM INTERNATIONAL DUTY

REBECCA HOLLOWAY
DEFENDER
RACING LOUISVILLE (USA)

MINUTES PLAYED AT EUROS
181

AGE 26   CAPS 14   GOALS 3

REBECCA McKENNA
DEFENDER
LEWES WOMEN

 MINUTES PLAYED AT EUROS
163

AGE 20   CAPS 25   GOALS 2

KELSIE BURROWS
DEFENDER
CLIFTONVILLE LADIES

 MINUTES PLAYED AT EUROS
89

AGE 21   CAPS 11   GOALS 0

ABBIE MAGEE
DEFENDER
CLIFTONVILLE LADIES

 MINUTES PLAYED AT EUROS
131

AGE 21   CAPS 11   GOALS 0

LAURA RAFFERTY
DEFENDER
SOUTHAMPTON WOMEN

 MINUTES PLAYED AT EUROS
66

AGE 26   CAPS 33   GOALS 0

DEMI VANCE
DEFENDER/MIDFIELDER
LEICESTER CITY WOMEN

 MINUTES PLAYED AT EUROS
270-PLUS

AGE 31   CAPS 81   GOALS 4

WAS ON VERGE OF LEAVING RANGERS WOMEN
AT EUROS, NOW WITH LEICESTER CITY WOMEN
IN WSL

SARAH McFADDEN
DEFENDER/MIDFIELDER
DURHAM WOMEN

 MINUTES PLAYED AT EUROS
270-PLUS

AGE 35   CAPS 95   GOALS 8

NADENE CALDWELL
MIDFIELDER
GLENTORAN WOMEN

 MINUTES PLAYED AT EUROS
55

AGE 31   CAPS 72   GOALS 2

RACHEL FURNESS
MIDFIELDER
LIVERPOOL WOMEN

 MINUTES PLAYED AT EUROS
233

AGE 34   CAPS 89   GOALS 38

MARISSA CALLAGHAN
MIDFIELDER
CLIFTONVILLE LADIES

 MINUTES PLAYED AT EUROS
217

AGE 36   CAPS 78   GOALS 9

CHLOE McCARRON
MIDFIELDER
GLENTORAN WOMEN

 MINUTES PLAYED AT EUROS
180

AGE 24   CAPS 28   GOALS 1

JOELY ANDREWS
MIDFIELDER
GLENTORAN WOMEN

 MINUTES PLAYED AT EUROS
11

AGE 20   CAPS 10   GOALS 1

LOUISE McDANIEL
MIDFIELDER
CLIFTONVILLE LADIES

 MINUTES PLAYED AT EUROS
5

AGE 22   CAPS 11   GOALS 1

SIMONE MAGILL
FORWARD
ASTON VILLA WOMEN

MINUTES PLAYED AT EUROS
79

| AGE 27 | CAPS 70 | GOALS 21 |

HAD JUST LEFT EVERTON WOMEN BEFORE EUROS,
NOW WITH ASTON VILLA WOMEN IN WSL

LAUREN WADE
FORWARD
READING WOMEN

MINUTES PLAYED AT EUROS
260

| AGE 28 | CAPS 45 | GOALS 7 |

WITH GLENTORAN WOMEN AT EUROS, NOW WITH
READING IN WSL

KIRSTY McGUINNESS
FORWARD
CLIFTONVILLE LADIES

MINUTES PLAYED AT EUROS
185

| AGE 27 | CAPS 63 | GOALS 14 |

CAITLIN McGUINNESS
FORWARD
CLIFTONVILLE LADIES

MINUTES PLAYED AT EUROS
16

| AGE 19 | CAPS 16 | GOALS 1 |

EMILY WILSON
FORWARD
CRUSADERS STRIKERS

MINUTES PLAYED AT EUROS
24

| AGE 20 | CAPS 16 | GOALS 1 |

THE BIG SEND-OFF

The Northern Ireland squad, manager and backroom staff met at the Culloden Hotel in Cultra, Co Down, to pose for official send-off photographs prior to their departure to the tournament on a charter flight to Southampton.

WORKING BEHIND THE SCENES

Intense planning for the team's participation at the Euros began within the Irish Football Association in early December 2021.

Immediately after the draw and finding out that all three group matches would be played in Southampton, David Currie (Head of International Department) and Heather Wright (International Teams Administrator) set off on a site visit to the port city on England's South Coast to assess the facilities and decide on what would be the most suitable set-up for a team base camp.

In addition a Women's Euro 2022 planning group was formed with operational staff to organise staff and see to the needs of all involved.

This group consisted of Angela Platt (Director of Women's Football), Peter Gilpin (Project Manager), Karen Dunne (Project Officer), David Currie, Stephen Grange (Security Officer), Stephen Bogle (Head of Sales and Marketing) and Danny Lynch (Director of Communications).

Project Manager Peter Gilpin explained: "This was the kick-off for what would be eight months of planning to take the team and Irish FA support staff to the final tournament.

"While the squad, Kenny (Shiels) and his backroom team were preparing in the full-time training programme at Newforge, operational planning was taking place behind the scenes looking at all aspects of competing in a UEFA final tournament.

"Focusing on the team operations, a plan was put in place with the Harbour Hotel in Southampton to create a comfortable and homely environment where the players and staff would have the best opportunity to prepare for their fixtures."

He explained several site visits took place in the run-up to the tournament to look at how the 'living space' would be created.

"A standout feature was the players' recreation area with pool tables, dart boards, table tennis tables, games consoles, TVs and board games, which was described by UEFA Team Service as the best team facility they had seen," he revealed.

Inside the hotel 'A New Dream' branding and messaging featured throughout the designated team areas, creating a special atmosphere for the players to live in. Qualifying campaign imagery featured throughout, with personal photographs and bespoke gifts placed in bedrooms for players and team staff to enjoy.

The team training centre was located at Stoneham Lane Football Complex, a Hampshire FC-owned facility approximately 15 minutes' drive from the team hotel.

Peter said: "The team had exclusive use of the complex for the duration of their stay on the South Coast and although the summer drought didn't help the training pitch it was an ideal set-up to prepare for each match.

"At the training base we created a Northern Ireland Media Centre for daily press conferences and other media activities which was ably set up by Thomas Fulton and Richard Currie from the association's IT department, with James Courtney and his Signstik colleagues branding it with lots of Irish FA logos and pictures.

"Individual pictures of each player in the squad adorned the walls of the media centre to give that special feeling when players were undertaking press activities.

"To facilitate the set-up a 45 ft lorry packed with equipment and supplies left Belfast days before the team and was met in Southampton by David Currie, Karen Dunne, Thomas Fulton, Richard Currie and myself, and we spent three days setting up prior to the travelling party's arrival."

The team and the rest of the travelling party flew out of Belfast City Airport to Southampton where they were greeted on the apron of the runway by a Women's Euro branded team bus. The vehicle, with the words 'Northern Ireland' writ large on its front, back and sides, took them straight to the team hotel to officially start their UEFA Women's Euro 2022 adventure.

Other staff who helped out on the South Coast included Glenda Dines, who looked after transport, and Rachel Logan, who managed VIPs and protocol. Norrie Clarke and Stevie Garrett were responsible for fan engagement, while the association's communications team (Danny Lynch, Nigel Tilson, John Gillespie, Andy McComb and Ciaran Quinn) plus photographer William Cherry promoted the team widely in the media and on social media.

KENNY SHIELS' BACKROOM TEAM AT THE EUROS

Dean Shiels
Assistant Manager

Dwayne Nelson
Goalkeeping Coach

William Wilson
Team Doctor

Catherine Ferguson
Physiotherapist

Dervla Murphy
Physiotherapist

Jonny Pedlow
Strength & Conditioning
Coach/Kitman

Ewelina Tomasiack
Masseuse

Damian McCarry
Team Analyst

Stevie Ferguson
Kitman

Heather Wright
Team Administration

UEFA WOMEN'S EURO 2022
GROUP A

NORWAY 4
J. BLAKSTAD (10'), F. MAANUM (13'),
C. HANSEN (PEN 31'), G. REITEN (54')

NORTHERN IRELAND 1
J. NELSON (49')

THURSDAY 7 JULY 2022
ST MARY'S STADIUM, SOUTHAMPTON
KICK-OFF 20.00
ATTENDANCE: 9,146

NORWEGIANS TURN ON STYLE IN HISTORIC GAME

Norway were too hot to handle as Northern Ireland's senior women's team made their bow at a major tournament.

In warm and balmy conditions at St Mary's Stadium in Southampton, Norway showed their class against Kenny Shiels' side, producing plenty of slick attacking play as they notched up a 4-1 victory.

Defender/midfielder Sarah McFadden captained her country in the historic game.

McFadden, who had led the team against Norway home and away in the qualifiers for the tournament, was given the armband because there were concerns that Marissa Callaghan, the squad captain, had

not sufficiently recovered from a toe injury to take her place in the starting line-up. Callaghan did enter the fray, however, for the second half.

In the match Northern Ireland were constantly put under pressure by Norway, who had two superstars of the women's game in their ranks – Lyon forward Ada Hegerberg and Barcelona winger Caroline Graham Hansen.

The start to the first group game in the tournament for both sides was cagey as they eased their way into the game in front of just over 9,000 fans.

Guro Reiten slipped the ball to Hegerberg, however McFadden put the Norway forward under pressure and she fired her shot well over the top.

A Rachel Furness cross into the area was cleared before Reiten headed over the top at the other end.

Norway opened the scoring on 10 minutes when the lively Reiten fed Julie Blakstad down the left and she stroked the ball into the bottom corner. It was a clinical finish.

Minutes later attacking midfielder Furness let fly from long range, however her effort was off target.

Northern Ireland keeper Jackie Burns saved well from Frida Maanum before Norway went two up. Chloe McCarron was robbed by Maanum just outside the area and the midfielder played a one-two with Hegerberg before clipping the ball home.

On 22 minutes Burns saved well from Amalie Eikeland and then she pushed a fine long range effort from Maanum around the post. And Hegerberg headed wide as Norway continued to turn the screw

Abbie Magee battled for possession on the edge of the area and poked the ball to Lauren Wade whose drive went wide of the post. Magee was quickly back on defensive duty to repel another Norwegian raid.

Norway were awarded a penalty when Nadene Caldwell was adjudged to have handled the ball in the area as she tried to clear a Reiten corner. Following a VAR check, Finnish referee Lina Lehtovaara said the ball had hit Caldwell's elbow and pointed to the

spot on 31 minutes. Player of the match Caroline Graham Hansen blasted the spot kick past Burns.

McFadden and her fellow centre back Julie Nelson continued to thwart attacks as Norway piled forward.

Burns produced a couple of saves before, on the stroke of half-time, Northern Ireland striker Simone Magill fizzed a shot wide.

Northern Ireland pulled one back just after the break when a Demi Vance delivery from a corner caused confusion in the Norway box and Furness eventually lofted the ball to the back post where Nelson was lurking to nod the ball home - and make history by becoming the first Northern Ireland senior women's international to score at a major tournament.

Martin Sjogren's team almost responded immediately, however Magee managed to clear the danger as Hegerberg fired the ball goalwards.

Wade shot straight at Norwegian keeper Guro Pettersen as Northern Ireland enjoyed a rare spell of possession.

Norway scored their fourth thanks to a sublime free-kick. McFadden conceded a foul on the edge of the area and Reiten stepped up to curl the ball around the wall into the bottom corner.

Marissa Callaghan, the captain of the Northern Ireland squad, entered the fray at the start of the second half and was quickly on the ball. A probing pass put Wade clear down the right, but the danger was snuffed out.

Chances were few and far between as both sides made substitutions. And in the 78th minute Northern Ireland lost striker Simone Magill through injury. It was later confirmed she had damaged the anterior cruciate ligament in her left knee, which meant she could play no further part in the tournament.

In the closing stages Burns produced another fine save to deny Norway substitute Karina Saevik.

On netting Northern Ireland's goal Julie Nelson, at the age of 37 years and 33 days, became the oldest scorer at a Euros; she broke a record held by Italy legend Patrizia Panico since 2009.

NORWAY (4-2-3-1)

Guro Pettersen, Anja Sonstevold (Tuva Hansen 65'), Maria Thorisdottir, Julie Blakstad (Anna Josendal 89'), Maren Mjelde (captain) (Guro Birgsvand 81'), Frida Maanum (Vilda Boa Risa 65'), Ingrid Syrstad Engen, Amalie Eikeland (Karina Saevik 65'), Ada Hegerberg, Caroline Graham Hansen, Guro Reiten

Subs not used Sunniva Skoglund (GK), Aurora Mikalsen (GK), Celin Ildhusoy, Thea Bjelde, Elisabeth Terland, Synne Hansen, Sophie Haug

NORTHERN IRELAND (3-4-2-1)

Jackie Burns, Abbie Magee, Kelsie Burrows (Rebecca Holloway 65'), Sarah McFadden (captain), Julie Nelson, Nadene Caldwell (Marissa Callaghan 46'), Chloe McCarron, Rachel Furness (Kirsty McGuinness 74'), Simone Magill (Caitlin McGuinness 79'), Lauren Wade (Emily Wilson 80'), Demi Vance

Subs not used Becky Flaherty (GK), Shannon Turner (GK), Rebecca McKenna, Ashley Hutton, Laura Rafferty, Louise McDaniel, Joely Andrews

Booked Sarah McFadden (53')

Referee Lina Lehtovaara (Finland)

UEFA WOMEN'S EURO 2022
GROUP A

AUSTRIA 2
K. SCHIECHTL (19'), K. NASCHENWENG (88')

NORTHERN IRELAND 0

MONDAY 11 JULY 2022
ST MARY'S STADIUM, SOUTHAMPTON
KICK-OFF 17:00
ATTENDANCE 9,268

AUSTRIANS SCORE LATE IN NARROW VICTORY

Northern Ireland were narrowly defeated 2-0 by Austria in their second group game at UEFA Women's Euro 2022.

They worked tirelessly in front of over 9,000 fans at St Mary's, however they could not find a reply to Austria, who scored in the first half before sealing the win late on.

The defeat meant Northern Ireland could not qualify from the group even if they won their final group fixture.

Showing four changes from the starting 11 against Norway, Kenny Shiels' side battled for everything and were unfortunate not to take something from the game.

Simone Magill, who exited the tournament after damaging her knee in the first group match, was a big loss. The team undoubtedly missed her relentless running into the channels and her excellent hold-up play.

After an even start Austria started to push forward and winger Julia Hickelsberger-Fuller put a header wide in the seventh minute.

Northern Ireland winger Lauren Wade produced a fine run down the right but was eventually stopped in her tracks. And on the other flank Kirsty McGuinness also had a penetrating run which was snuffed out before Hickelsberger-Fuller put an effort into the side netting.

Wade cut inside and fired in a shot which was comfortably held by Austria keeper Manuela Zinsberger.

Northern Ireland goalie Jackie Burns made a couple of saves as the Austrians began to up the tempo in the sweltering conditions. The temperature gauge was at 35c pitchside just before kick-off.

Austria took the lead on 19 minutes. Midfielder Sarah Puntigam drove in a free-kick which took a deflection off Julie Nelson in the two-man wall and was tucked home by alert Austrian defender Katharina Schiechtl from four yards.

Sarah McFadden, who had by that stage already produced several blocks, raced back to clear the danger as Austria threatened once more.

Austria continued to enjoy the bulk of possession, spraying the ball around and stretching the Northern Ireland midfield and defence.

Demi Vance lifted a cross into the area which was controlled by captain Marissa Callaghan, however she could not get a shot away.

A loose clearance from Burns fell to player of the match Barbara Dunst who curled the ball goalwards and Burns had to react quickly to push her effort onto the bar. It was a super save.

McFadden appeared to be pushed in the back as Vance delivered a corner, however Venezualan referee Emikar Barrera waved the penalty appeals away.

As half-time approached Rebecca Holloway fed McGuinness who let fly from outside the area, however the ball was clutched by Zinsberger.

At the start of the second half Vance and McGuinness got in behind the Austrian defence with some neat interplay, however Vance was blocked off as she tried to trick her way into the box. And then Wade lofted an effort over the bar.

Austria midfielder Sarah Zadrazil, who was a constant threat with her bursts from deep, shot into the side netting

In the 64th minute a rising Dunst snapshot was fumbled by Burns and dropped on to the top of the net.

Minutes later Callaghan fed McGuinness and she jinked past a couple of markers before her cross was cleared.

Rachel Furness, who had been having a quiet match by her standards, sprang to life to guide a header on to the top of the net as Northern Ireland applied pressure.

A McGuinness cross was comfortably held by Zinsberger before the second water break of the game.

Substitute Katharina Naschenweng made sure of all three points for Austria when she added a second two minutes from time, clinically drilling the ball across goal past Burns into the bottom corner.

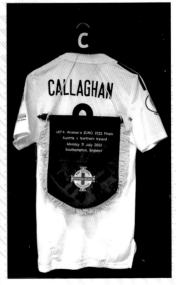

AUSTRIA (4-4-2)

Manuela Zinsberger, Verena Hanshaw, Katharina Schiechtl, Viki Schnaderbeck (captain) (Marina Georgieva 46'), Carina Wenninger, Julia Hickelsberger-Fuller (Katharina Naschenweng 73'), Sarah Puntigam, Barbara Dunst, Nicole Billa (Lisa Makas 85'), Marie Hobinger (Laura Feiersinger 46'), Sarah Zadrazil

Subs not used Isabella Kresche (GK), Jasmin Pal (GK), Celina Degen, Annabel Schasching, Virginia Kirchberger, Jasmin Eder, Stefanie Enzinger

NORTHERN IRELAND (3-4-2-1)

Jackie Burns, Rebecca McKenna (Abbie Magee 73'), Demi Vance, Sarah McFadden, Julie Nelson (Louise McDaniel 85'), Rebecca Holloway, Chloe McCarron, Marissa Callaghan (captain) (Caitlin McGuinness 85'), Kirsty McGuinness (Emily Wilson 79'), Rachel Furness (Joely Andrews 79'), Lauren Wade

Subs not used Becky Flaherty (GK), Shannon Turner (GK), Ashley Hutton, Kelsie Burrows, Nadene Caldwell, Laura Rafferty

Referee Emikar Calderas Barrera (Venezuala)

REPORT MARTIN HARRIS & NIGEL TILSON

LIONESSES BARE THEIR TEETH IN FIVE-GOAL TRIUMPH

Northern Ireland's involvement in their first major tournament ended with a defeat at the hands of UEFA Women's Euro 2022 hosts and eventual winners England.

Kenny Shiels' side worked their socks off in the game, however the Lionesses were in no mood to take their foot off the gas in pursuit of topping the group - and they triumphed thanks to some excellent finishes.

Northern Ireland had the first chance of the game though. As early as the opening minute Lauren Wade worked her way through the England defence to force keeper Mary Earps into a good save.

Then Jackie Burns was called into action to punch the ball clear as England striker Ellen White looked set to pounce.

England were awarded a penalty after six minutes following a decision by Swiss referee Esther Staubli but a VAR check reversed that and, indeed, the incident ended with an indirect free-kick for Northern Ireland after it was shown that England's Beth Mead had handled the ball moments before.

The hungry Lionesses upped the tempo and pushed forward. Burns did well once more to block a Georgia Stanway effort with her legs.

Rebecca Holloway sliced open the England defence but, despite connecting with the ball, Wade couldn't get enough purchase to make the opportunity count.

England had the bulk of the possession. Julie Nelson blocked a Mead shot and Burns smothered a Stanway effort.

The chances continued with White latching on to a Lucy Bronze pass, however she screwed her shot wide.

Then, with six minutes of the first half remaining, Holloway was in the right place to stop a Stanway attempt on the line.

Northern Ireland's defence was breached just 60 seconds after that though. A Lauren Hemp shot was blocked, however the ball dropped outside the area for Fran Kirby to side foot it into the top corner beyond the reach of Burns. It was a lovely finish.

England doubled their lead moments before the break. A corner was not properly cleared and the ball fell to Lauren Hemp whose low strike flew into the bottom corner.

Sarina Wiegman's side added a third three minutes after the interval. Alessia Russo, one of three substitutes to enter the fray at the start of the second half, made her mark with a clever cushioned header into the bottom corner from Mead's crisp delivery.

Russo extended England's advantage further just four minutes later with a superb finish. She received the ball from Ella Toone with her back to goal and turned her marker before running forward and slotting the ball past Burns.

There was further pain for Northern Ireland on 76 minutes when Kelsie Burrows turned the ball into her own net as she stuck a leg out to try to stop a Mead cross. The ball looped over Burns and dropped into the net.

Player of the match Russo had opportunities to complete her hat-trick late in the game, however the Northern Ireland defence managed to keep her at bay.

It was an emphatic victory for the Lionesses, who enjoyed 78% possession in the match. And they would go on to defeat Germany 2-1 after extra time in the final at Wembley thanks to goals from Ella Toone and Chloe Kelly, both of whom came on as second half subs in the game against Northern Ireland.

Shiels' charges could rightly hold their heads high afterwards. They put in a gutsy performance against a world class team.

They also enjoyed quite a party with the Green and White Army at the end of the encounter. And several England players acknowledged the incredible support for Shiels' team in the stadium. As they made their way off the pitch they applauded the Northern Ireland fans in the stands.

After the match veteran defender Ashley Hutton announced her retirement from international football. She said playing at the Euros was a fitting way to bring the curtain down. Ashley earned 115 caps for her country across almost two decades.

ENGLAND (3-4-2-1)

Mary Earps, Lucy Bronze (Jess Carter 74'), Millie Bright (Alex Greenwood 46'), Leah Williamson (captain), Rachel Daly, Georgia Stanway (Ella Toone 46'), Keira Walsh, Beth Mead, Fran Kirby, Lauren Hemp (Chloe Kelly 60'), Ellen White (Alessia Russo 46')

Subs not used Hannah Hampton (GK), Ellie Roebuck (GK), Lotte Wubben-Moy, Bethany England, Jill Scott, Nikita Parris

NORTHERN IRELAND (3-4-2-1)

Jackie Burns, Rebecca McKenna, Julie Nelson (Ashley Hutton 87'), Sarah McFadden, Laura Rafferty (Kelsie Burrows 66'), Demi Vance, Rebecca Holloway (Abbie Magee 66'), Lauren Wade, Marissa Callaghan (captain) (Emily Wilson 87'), Kirsty McGuinness, Rachel Furness (Nadene Caldwell 80')

Subs not used Becky Flaherty (GK), Shannon Turner (GK), Joely Andrews, Caitlin McGuinness, Louise McDaniel, Chloe McCarron

Referee Esther Staubli (Switzerland)

FACING THE MEDIA

Press conferences were staged regularly during the group stages at Women's Euro 2022.

The Northern Ireland manager and team captain faced the media at St Mary's Stadium in Southampton the day before each match (known as matchday minus one in UEFA circles), while the manager attended a press conference in the stadium after each game.

In the run-up to the three matches, players within the squad were chosen, in pairs, to face the media at a press conference room created at the Stoneham Lane training complex.

The room was suitably branded with Irish FA logos and pictures of the players. It was well received by visiting media. A media working room was also provided next door to the press conference room. Broadcast media conducted interviews with the players in and around the complex.

Prior to the squad departing for the Euros a media access day was staged at the National Football Stadium at Windsor Park. This enabled broadcast media and written press to interview all the players in a relaxed environment. Photographers and videographers from UEFA also attended the event to capture footage for uefa.com and UEFA TV.

On their final day at the Stoneham Lane complex the squad signed the pictures that adorned the interior walls and took selfies with themselves!

'A NEW DREAM' SCREENED IN SOUTHAMPTON

The Irish FA's short film which charted the behind-the-scenes story of Northern Ireland's historic qualification for UEFA Women's Euro 2022 was screened in Southampton prior to the team's second group game at the tournament.

The Harbour Lights Picture House in the port city hosted the special screening of 'A New Dream'.

Produced and edited by the association, the mini documentary captures the build-up to the Euro play-off matches against Ukraine in Kovalivka and Belfast and the celebrations afterwards.

At the special screening members of the senior women's team met up with family, friends and fans who had made their way to Southampton for Northern Ireland's games in the tournament.

'A New Dream', which was originally unveiled in 2021 and can be viewed on the Northern Ireland YouTube channel, provides a fascinating insight into Kenny Shiels' side's magnificent achievement against the odds.

THE SEQUEL

A sequel is set to be unveiled by the end of 2022 on the Northern Ireland YouTube channel.

Once again produced and edited by the Irish FA, with Andy 'Spielberg' McComb and Ciaran Quinn from the digital team pulling the strings in the engine room, with support from John Gillespie, David Cavan, William Cherry and Thomas Fulton (drone specialist), 'Why We Dance' charts the behind-the-scenes story of the senior women's team's participation at Women's Euro 2022.

'Why We Dance' was premiered at a special screening for fans at Belfast's Strand Cinema.

EUROS SHOW IS A HIT

In the run-up to the Women's Euros the Irish FA's communications team launched a three-part online series featuring some Northern Ireland senior women's team players.

'We're On Our Way' saw guest presenter Helen Evans travel around the UK to chat to six players.

She met Chloe McCarron and Lauren Wade in Belfast before a hop over the Irish Sea to Scotland to chat to Demi Vance and Megan Bell. Then it was down to Liverpool to meet up with Rachel Furness and Simone Magill.

The show was aired exclusively on Northern Ireland's social media channels across YouTube, Facebook and Twitter.

And when it came to the tournament itself Helen teamed up with Andy McComb and Ciaran Quinn from the Irish FA's digital team to create 'We're On Our Way – At The Euros'.

The three-part series, which was again shown exclusively on Northern Ireland channels, featured relaxed sit-down interviews with players and fan-focused content. In a couple of the shows players showed off their golf skills to win prizes for fans who attended the games in Southampton.

Midfielders Nadene Caldwell and Joely Andrews took part in the first show, while young strikers Emily Wilson and Caitlin McGuinness were game for a laugh in the second show.

The final show featured Caragh Hamilton, who missed out on playing in the tournament through injury but excelled as a TV pundit, and superfan Gemma Garrett.

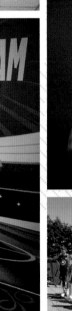
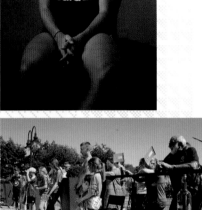

ON LOCATION

William Cherry (Press Eye) went 'on location' within Southampton to find backdrops for special feature pictures of players which were used by both print and online media globally during the tournament. Louise McDaniel, Kelsie Burrows and team mascot Sweet Caroline all featured in the photoshoots

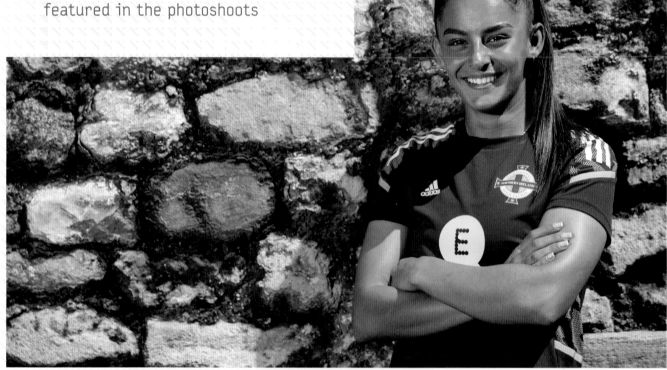

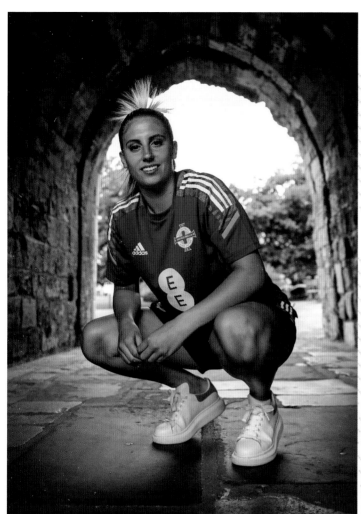

SARAH McFADDEN

WHO CAPTAINED THE TEAM IN THE GAME AGAINST NORWAY

"The Euros was incredible from the moment we boarded the plane in our lovely M&S suits until the moment we left Southampton and returned home to our families.

"Never in my career did I think we would qualify for a tournament, so before the tournament my brother-in-law sent me a video about enjoying the whole experience and not putting any pressure on myself when playing.

"It said to look back with no regrets because you may never get this experience again and that's how I feel now. I loved it. I got to compete with the best in the world and play in front of the most amazing fans and I will remember those moments forever.

"When Kenny asked me to be captain for the first game I was gutted for Marissa (who had only just recovered from a toe injury) and would have preferred to have walked out behind her because she is our captain.

"I will probably never truly appreciate that moment until I am retired and can show my daughter Harper that her mum was the first person to captain Northern Ireland at their first major championships, and I hope she thinks that's pretty amazing."

"Qualifying for our first major tournament was my dream from the very first moment I had the privilege to pull on a green shirt.

"Against all the odds, in typical underdog fashion, we achieved what nobody thought was possible.

"Getting there has been the biggest highlight of my career to date and I hope it's the first of many more for our wee country."

SIMONE MAGILL

RACHEL FURNESS

"Qualifying for the Euros was a lifelong dream of mine.

"The first time I put on that Northern Ireland shirt I thought I would only ever dream of playing in a major tournament.

"Through the ups and downs to see us inspire made it all worth it. was for those who came before us and those who will be lucky en to come after us. We're Northern Ireland, history makers. Be prou

"Qualifying for the European Championships will be a moment I will remember forever. For a little country to qualify for a major tournament, it was something special.

"We believed from the very start we could do it, but we were the only ones. No-one else believed we could.

"The tournament was amazing and it was great to have so many of the GAWA there to support us through it all."

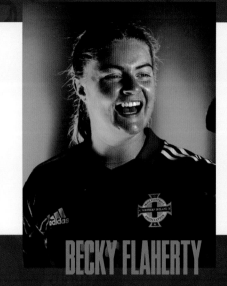

BECKY FLAHERTY

CHLOE McCARRON

"'From the moment we qualified after the Ukraine game to actually being at the tournament was surreal. There were 16 teams in the finals and we were one of them, which is crazy!

"A big part of the experience was the fans. I can't believe how much our fan base has grown from the start of the qualifiers until now.

"This really hit home after our last game at the Euros against England when we as players shared a great moment with the fans. To be a part of the first women's Northern Ireland team at a major tournament is something I will always be proud of. It makes me want to get to another major tournament with this team."

JACKIE BURNS

"Being involved in one of the most historic moments in Northern Ireland women's football was unforgettable. When that final whistle went at Seaview (after the second leg of the play-off), that moment was priceless. Hearing the car horns blaring outside the ground, since we were following Covid protocols at the time, was a unique way to remember that night. We had the support even though they couldn't physically be there in person.

"When the Euros finally came, we savoured every moment. Walking out on the pitch for each game was special. The GAWA made that place (St Mary's) our home."

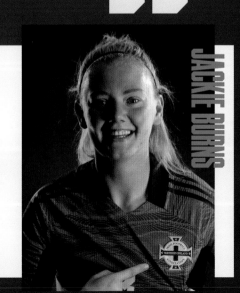

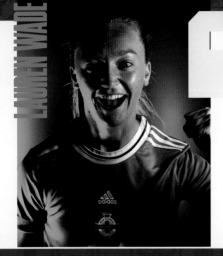

LAUREN WADE

"The moment the final whistle went (after the second leg of the play-off) was a feeling I can't describe. To have qualified for our first major tournament and to create history with this special group was a dream come true. From the first game of the campaign to the last we always had the belief that our dreams could become reality.

"The Euros is something I'll remember for the rest of my life. The feeling of walking out for each game and hearing the GAWA is something I'll never forget. The support was unbelievable. We will be forever grateful to Kenny and his coaching staff for all they have done for all of us. What an unforgettable experience!"

"From qualifying in an empty Seaview stadium to playing in front of 35,000 people in Southampton felt like a dream.

"To have this experience with your team mates who are your closest friends is something I'll remember forever. Our manager Kenny and coaching staff gave us the belief to achieve what we thought was impossible. For that we will be forever grateful."

DEMI VANCE

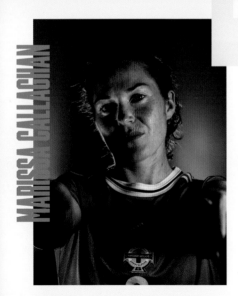

MARISSA CALLAGHAN

CAPTAIN - WHO LED THE TEAM OUT FOR TWO MATCHES

"Qualifying for our first major tournament with this squad of players and staff will always be the best few years of my playing career.

"Looking back we had so many defining moments, the highs, the lows and everything in between. Ashley Hutton's equaliser against Wales, Furney's header v Belarus, scoring myself against Ukraine to help us win our play-off. The hard times came through injury. Seeing team-mates miss out on squads was heartbreaking.

"Our qualification journey to the European Championship finals has changed the face of women's football forever in our wee country.

"I am so grateful to have led this team of amazing women out in our first major finals as captain.

"Every single player gave their all and I hope this will be the beginning of something special for females in Northern Ireland to have the dedication and belief that we can compete against the big nations and that we are good enough.

"A big thank you has to go to our amazing fans. They were our 12th player during the Euros and I will never forget our dance at the end of the England game. Getting to the Euros was like winning it for us and I am so thankful we got to share it with them."

"The Euro play-off (second leg) against Ukraine at Seaview is a night that will live with all of us forever. Not only did we create history qualifying for our first major tournament, our dreams became reality.

"Representing Northern Ireland at the Euros is a moment I will never forget. The feeling of walking out of the tunnel with not only team-mates but friends and hearing the GAWA was just incredible.

"The support we felt was unbelievable and we hope it has inspired a new generation to dream big."

NADENE CALDWELL

JOELY ANDREWS

"Representing Northern Ireland at a major tournament as part of a history-making squad was something I never thought possible.

"Walking out in front of the Green and White Army at St Mary's was a dream come true. We were all so proud hearing the fans sing from minute one to 90.

"The most special part of the whole tournament was having family and friends there to support us. Singing with them after the England game was a massive highlight."

"To go from kicking a ball around in Sandy Bay playing fields in Larne as a young girl, completely oblivious of the opportunities that lay ahead, to having the honour of representing Northern Ireland 130 times has been truly special.

"From paying to go to our first Algarve Cup in 2004 to buying our own training kit and travelling throughout Europe with many more losses than victories, it's been an absolute whirlwind.

"All of those sacrifices, over so many years, have all been worth it to represent our wee country, and stepping on to the pitch at St Mary's Stadium at UEFA Women's Euro 2022 has been the highlight to date.

"If you had been drawing up a list of potential scorers for Northern Ireland at Euro 2022, my name would not have been high up the list. To make history and score that goal was incredible.

"That euphoric feeling is something that will stay with me for the rest of my life. What a special moment to share with this remarkable group, my family and, of course, the amazing Green and White Army - 7th July 2022 is a date that I will never forget."

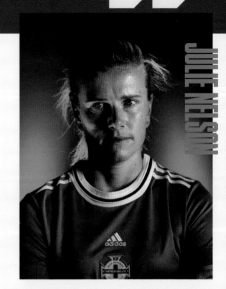

JULIE NELSON

SCORER OF THAT HISTORIC GOAL

GROWING THE FAN BASE

For years a superfan called Shaun Schofield would be the only fan in the stands when the Northern Ireland senior women's team played away from home.

And during the Covid pandemic lockdowns - when international sports teams were given special permission by governments to compete if they followed strict testing regimes - only the 'Tilson Gulder' could be heard when the team took to the pitch home and away.

These days it's different. The Northern Ireland team's success on the pitch has attracted a growing fan base and the Green and White Army - the family division in particular - are now supporting them on a much larger scale.

The Women's World Cup qualifier against England in April 2022 attracted a record crowd for a home senior women's international match, with more than 15,000 fans packing in to the National Football Stadium at Windsor Park to watch it.

Thousands of fans followed the senior women's team at the Euros and they created an incredible atmosphere during all three games in Southampton.

FIFA WOMEN'S WORLD CUP 2023 QUALIFIER (EUROPEAN GROUP D)

LUXEMBOURG 1
A. THOMPSON (80')

NORTHERN IRELAND 2
S. McFADDEN (52'), R. McKENNA (85')

FRIDAY 2 SEPTEMBER 2022
STADE ÉMILE MAYRISCH, ESCH-SUR-ALZETTE.
KICK-OFF 17:30

BACK TO WINNING WAYS

Following their Euros adventure Northern Ireland got back to winning ways with a narrow 2-1 victory over Luxembourg.

Second half goals from Sarah McFadden and Rebecca McKenna were enough to secure all three points.

It could have been more comfortable for Kenny Shiels' side, who spurned several chances in the game.

But the win meant Northern Ireland finished third in European Group D in the qualifiers for next year's global tournament in Australia and New Zealand.

The result also meant Northern Ireland tasted victory again after their six defeats in a row against top tier teams in the run-up to and at UEFA Women's Euro 2022.

LUXEMBOURG (4-4-2)

L. Schlime, K. Dos Santos, C. Have, E. Kremer, N. Tiberi (J. Becker 65'), C. Jorge (J. Marques 73'), L. Miller, M. Soares (K. Mendes 65'), A. Thompson, C. Schmit (J. Lourenco 83'), M. Garcia (N. Ludwig 83')

Subs not used A. Weyer (GK), E. Goetz (GK), I. Albert, M. Schon, A. Delgado, M. Lourenco, E. Kocan

Booked M. Garcia (39'), J. Becker (71'), A. Thompson (74')

Sent Off A. Thompson (81')

NORTHERN IRELAND (4-4-2)

J. Burns, J. Nelson, S. McFadden, D. Vance, R. McKenna, L. McDaniel (C. Hamilton 46'), C. McGuinness, M. Callaghan (A. Magee 82'), C. McCarron (N. Caldwell 46'), J. Andrews (R. Holloway 46'), K. McGuinness

Subs not used S. Turner (GK), L. Woods (GK), L. Wade, T. Finnegan, E. Mason, G. McKimm, E. Wilson, K. Beattie

Referee J. Pejkovic (Croatia)

TRIO OF OWN GOALS HELPS NORTHERN IRELAND CREATE HISTORY

Northern Ireland had to come from behind to secure a 3-1 win against Latvia in their final FIFA Women's World Cup 2023 qualifier.

FIFA WOMEN'S WORLD CUP 2023 QUALIFIER (EUROPEAN GROUP D)

LATVIA 1
A. ROCANE (27')

NORTHERN IRELAND 3
E. VAIVODE (OG 36', OG 90+5'), A. LUBINA (OG 88')

TUESDAY 6 SEPTEMBER 2022
SLOKAS STADIONA, JURMALA
KICK-OFF 15:00

Amazingly all three of Northern Ireland's goals were scored by the opposition. Latvia keeper Enija-Anna Vaivode notched two of them, while the other was netted by defender Arta Luize Lubina.

The victory meant Kenny Shiels' side created history. It brought their points tally in European Group D to 19 – a record haul for a qualification campaign involving the senior women's team.

It was a bizarre end to a campaign which saw Northern Ireland finish in third place in European Group D behind table toppers England and Austria. The hope is that the impressive points haul will be enough to improve Northern Ireland's co-efficient for future competitions.

LATVIA (3-5-2)

E. Vaivode, S. Voitane, A. Lubina, A. Rocane, A. Poluhovica, A. Gornela, T. Smirnova (V. Zaicikova 54'), K. Miksone, N. Treimane, K. Danilova (R. Fedotova 54'), O. Sevcova.

Subs not used A. Sklemenova (GK), S. Nesterova (GK), S. Senberga, E. Druvina, S. Vitmore, E. Freidenfelde, K. Lodzina, K. Zacmane, S. Garanca

Booked K. Miksone (79')

NORTHERN IRELAND (4-1-4-1)

J. Burns, R. McKenna, S. McFadden, E. Mason (K. McGuinness 69'), D. Vance, T. Finnegan (A. Magee 68'), C. Hamilton, N. Caldwell, M. Callaghan (R. Holloway 69'), E. Wilson (C. McCarron 69'), C. McGuinness (K. Beattie 82')

Subs not used S. Turner (GK), L. Woods (GK), L. Wade, G. McKimm, J. Andrews, J. Nelson, L. McDaniel

Booked N. Caldwell (26')

Referee K. Sipos (Hungary)

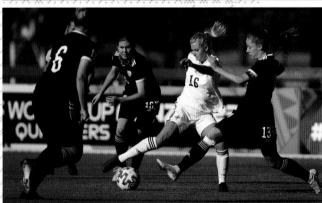

NORTHERN IRELAND PLAYERS ENJOY SPECIAL RECEPTIONS

Belfast's Lord Mayor, Councillor Tina Black, receives a Northern Ireland shirt from senior women's team manager Kenny Shiels as players (from left) Emily Wilson, Julie Nelson, team captain Marissa Callaghan and Demi Vance look on. Picture by Press Eye.

Belfast City Council recognised the achievements of the Northern Ireland senior women's team at a special reception in the City Hall in August.

Belfast's Lord Mayor, Councillor Tina Black, hosted the event, where she met manager Kenny Shiels and some of the players who represented Northern Ireland at UEFA Women's Euro 2022 in England.

The Lord Mayor said it was a pleasure to welcome the manager and squad members to City Hall and applauded the players for being part of the first senior women's team from Northern Ireland to reach a major tournament.

"It was an incredible achievement that will be an inspiration for young female footballers for generations," the Lord Mayor said.

Angela Platt, Director of Women's Football at the Irish Football Association, thanked Belfast City Council for recognising the team and the Lord Mayor for her interest in women's football.

And in October there was a civic reception for the players at Parliament Buildings in Stormont. Again it was held to recognise their achievements.

It was organised by the Department for Communities and it was attended by Northern Ireland Assembly members from all political parties.

Communities Minister Deirdre Hargey said: "I want to pay a special tribute to the women's senior football team for their performance on the international stage. It was a significant achievement to qualify for the UEFA Women's European Championship for the first time.

"Seeing local players engaging with purpose and passion at the highest level of European football has been an inspiration. They have shown young people that by getting involved, putting in the work, and believing in yourself, you can achieve your dreams."

Communities Minister Deirdre Hargey with Kenny Shiels, Northern Ireland players, team support staff and guests at the civic reception held at Parliament Buildings, Stormont. Picture by Brian Thompson.

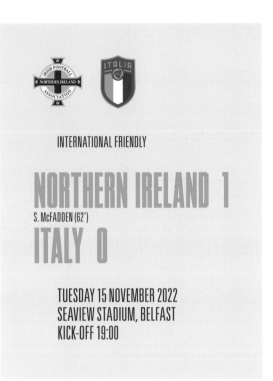

INTERNATIONAL FRIENDLY

NORTHERN IRELAND 1
S. McFADDEN (62')

ITALY 0

TUESDAY 15 NOVEMBER 2022
SEAVIEW STADIUM, BELFAST
KICK-OFF 19:00

FINE FRIENDLY WIN BRINGS MOMENTOUS YEAR TO A CLOSE

The senior women's team enjoyed an excellent victory over Italy in their final outing of 2022.

Kenny Shiels' side defeated the Italians 1-0 in an international challenge match at a packed Seaview in Belfast. Centre back Sarah McFadden, winning her 95th cap, scored the only goal of the mid-November game.

The Northern Ireland boss believes taking on stronger opponents is key to his players making further progress and they were more than up for the challenge against the Italians, who are ranked 14th in the world compared to Northern Ireland in 49th .

Both sides had chances before McFadden grabbed her goal on 62 minutes. A Demi Vance delivery from a corner found striker Emily Wilson and her close range effort was pushed out by the keeper but McFadden was on hand to poke the ball home from three yards.

NORTHERN IRELAND (4-2-3-1)

J. Burns, R. McKenna, D. Vance, S. McFadden
(J. Nelson 80'), K. Burrows, N. Caldwell
(J. Andrews 45'), C. McCarron (T. Finnegan 89'),
M. Callaghan (captain), E. Wilson (K. McGuinness
73'), C. Hamilton (L. McDaniel 73'), L. Wade
(C. McGuinness 72')

Subs not used S. Turner (GK), R. Holloway,
D. Maxwell, K. Beattie, A. Magee, F. Morgan

Booked J. Burns

ITALY (3-5-2)

L. Giuliani, F. Cafferata, E. Bartoli (B. Merlo 45'),
M. Luisa Filangeri, L. Boattin (E. Linari 71'), B.
Glionna (M. Giacinti 71'), M. Giugliano, F. Simonetti
(A. Caruso 71'), V. Cernoia (E. Polli 89'), B. Bonansea
(S. Cantore 34') , E. Bartoli

Subs not used R. Aprile (GK), A. Galli, M. Rosucci,
A. Soffia, F. Durante.

Referee V. De Cremer (Belgium)

PRESIDENT'S VIEW

2022 was a momentous year for women's football in Northern Ireland. The heroics of our senior women's team at the Euros inspired the nation.

The women's game here has gone from strength to strength. As interest continues in the wake of the Euros, perceptions have been changed and will change even further.

The attitude of the team, the relationship with the fans, the approach to women's football, we don't need to convince people anymore. The exploits of 2022 have moved the narrative from one of how far the women's game has come to one of just how far can it go.

Our 'A Roadmap for Football' strategy aims to recruit and retain women in coaching, match officiating and administration roles at all levels of the game – and to encourage participation among both girls and women.

Work on the legacy from the Euros must continue, and I will ensure that it does.

Conrad Kirkwood
President
Irish Football Association

NIGEL TILSON

Nigel Tilson is a senior media officer with the Irish Football Association.

He worked as a journalist for more than 25 years and is a former newspaper editor, business editor and sports editor. He has held senior positions in public relations since 2008. He also co-authored Dare To Dream, the book charting the Northern Ireland senior men's team's Euro 2016 adventure.

WILLIAM CHERRY

William Cherry is an award-winning senior photographer with Press Eye, a Belfast-based photo agency. He has been covering the Northern Ireland senior men's team's games for more than 30 years. His first away trip was in 1994 and he has travelled extensively with the team since then. In recent years he has also covered the senior women's team's matches home and away. Press Eye are the Irish FA's official photographers.

ACKNOWLEDGEMENTS

A huge 'thanks' to Northern Ireland's leading football stats man (Marshall Gillespie), my comms team colleagues at the Irish FA (who have to put up with all my stories; well, I am the elder statesman of the group and have been around a few corners!), the players, Kenny and Dean Shiels and the rest of the backroom team, Heather Wright (International Teams Administrator at the Irish FA), freelance writer Martin Harris, book cover designer and colleague Norman Boyd and Marty Manley (MAD Colour), who did a superb job on designing the rest of the book, and Gillian Cherry Fleming for creating the photo montages of fans from her brother's pictures. Plus anyone else who helped along the way. You know who you are!

And last but not least William Cherry. We worked together in newspaper land (Ulster Star in Lisburn) in the late 1980s. He was a cub photographer and I was a senior news reporter back then. He always had an eye for a good picture - and he has evolved into one of Northern Ireland's finest sports photographers. Thanks for your most excellent input William.

Nigel Tilson

IRISH FOOTBALL ASSOCIATION

President Conrad Kirkwood

Chief Executive Patrick Nelson

Official Publication by Irish Football Association
National Football Stadium at Windsor Park
Donegall Avenue, Belfast, BT12 9LW

Designed and printed by MAD Colour
401 Castlereagh Road, Belfast BT5 6QP